AF326632

STREAMS IN THE WILDERNESS

KAREN THOMPSON

DEDICATION

This book is dedicated to God, first and foremost, and to my husband and children, who light my life in ways they can't begin to imagine.

It is my act of obedience, my altar to God, marking the place in time where He revealed the depth of His love for me—healing deep and long-held wounds in my life—and where His kindness in a wilderness season revived my soul. He overwhelmed me with awe and wonder, and I stopped doubting how much He loved me. This love has a depth that I don't believe will ever be overturned in my life. These words serve as my record of His faithfulness to my family, something I believe He asked me to preserve for them, for generations to come, and anyone along the way who needs to hear it too. I know we are stronger together than apart.

And they overcame him by the blood of the Lamb and
by the word of their testimony.

— REVELATION 12:11 NKJV

CONTENTS

INTRODUCTION

Who am I? It's a question that might be asked on a game show, yet it's one I've avoided most of my life. I did not want to dig too deep to find an answer. Anyway, I was far too busy to take time to try—though it might be more honest to say that on some level I knew I wouldn't like what I might uncover.

When God moved our family to the United States in 2013 and my comfortable, familiar life and patterns were shaken, a wilderness engulfed me. It was a season that was harder than expected and took much longer than I thought we could survive. Yet, it gave me the opportunity to take the deep dive I so desperately avoided.

I grew up on the outer edges of a small village in Northern Ireland. You'd be wrong in thinking not much went on there because I grew up in a turbulent time of Northern Ireland's history known as "the Troubles." I folded a lot of abnormal events into daily life as the threat of paramilitary violence hung over our heads.

I don't remember being especially fearful of that, though. While I was shocked at times and saddened, I learned from observing and gleaning from conversations around me that if I didn't serve in any security services and knew which areas were safe to stick to, I'd most likely be okay.

To put it in the least complicated terms, as it's a complex subject, the battle raging in our province was ultimately for territory, but it also crossed religious lines. There were only a handful of schools not religiously segregated into either Protestant or Catholic, which helped compound hatred for many at an early age.

I often found myself thinking how sad this was because no one could help which side they were born on. When I was twelve years old, I experienced how my community reacted when I stood up for two young girls of the opposite religion who were spat on and screamed at on the school bus. These girls were not normally a stop on our route, and I have no idea why the driver picked them up that day, but of the forty or so other people on that bus, not a single person intervened.

Sitting at the halfway point of the bus, I knew there was going to be trouble because, as soon as the bus stopped, several older teenage boys seated at the back were already shouting in anger and calling them names. Once the girls got on, those same boys headed to the front where the girls stood to continue their abuse up close.

After several minutes, they came back to their seats, continuing to shout angry, abusive language toward the girls. I felt a sense of injustice rising within me. I kept hoping someone older, maybe a few others or even the bus driver, would at least attempt to ask the boys to stop, but I guess they all knew something I didn't.

After what felt like a long period of time, I decided enough was enough, and, with anxiety raging inside and my heart thumping, I dared to ask them to stop. As I sensed the air sucking out of the atmosphere around me, I immediately knew I was in trouble. Those seated near me seemed to sink uncomfortably deeper into their seats, sensing the repercussion to come in a way I did not.

I heard the footsteps and looked up to see the same boys standing by my seat, the ringleader and his two "bodyguards" (though what they thought a twelve-year-old girl could do to them, I don't know). Then, the leader grabbed my hair and yanked it back harshly. Holding my head back, he bent down to my ear and, in a low, sinister-sounding voice, informed me that if I ever stood up to them again, pulling my hair would be the least of my worries.

I'm not entirely sure what my fate would have been, but he did his job well because the threat was certainly enough to frighten me. What made the experience worse was the lack of support from anyone. It was like a dream or movie where everyone else in the scene blurs into the background and only you stand out. I felt so uncomfortably obvious. For the rest of the journey, I was almost scared to breathe—isolated and conflicted about the compassion I felt toward those girls, yet full of regret for being the one to speak up.

I understood better as I got older that lives were lost in our village, and feeling the pain of that can make itself evident in threatening, uncomfortable ways (not that it excuses the reactions, but it brings some understanding). Regardless of this, damage was done. Afterward, any time my mum sent me into the corner shop on an errand, I hated it because there always seemed to be a bunch of older teenage boys sitting on the windowsill outside, and I felt fearful and intimidated just by their presence.

Maybe that was the day—feeling intimidated, isolated, and conflicted by my feelings for justice—a seed was planted that Northern Ireland would not always be my home. A few years later, standing in a circle of friends outside the school tuck shop with a bag of my favorite prawn cocktail crisps in hand and listening to the general discussion of who thought they'd always live in Northern Ireland, I surprised myself by answering no. Perhaps my subconscious was verbalizing those feelings I'd held onto.

Despite the challenges, life in my family was fun (and it's them I credit with my sense of adventure). We lived on farmland given to my dad by my grandparents, a stone's throw away from their house, which was the hub of family gatherings. These moments together were loud and large, and I loved spending time with my aunts and cousins on our many adventures. Not that all our adventures went as smoothly as we hoped, though.

Like the day we went to the field with the river (the only field on my grandparents' property out of bounds to us) and almost lost our younger cousin. We stepped into the shallow part, thinking there was no harm, but it rained heavily for days before, and as we got carried away having fun, we didn't realize how deep we got in.

We were terrified when my youngest cousin started shouting for help as he lost his footing, and the current began to carry him away from us. Thankfully, his older brother, the swimmer among us, jumped in upstream to grab him. We thought we got away with it until my granny found the wet clothes stuffed in one of the small ovens in her AGA to dry!

When my dad met Jesus, our lives changed to a different kind of adventure. In our home, alcohol and cigarettes were replaced with the Bible, and conversations were different, as Dad talked fervently and passionately about his encounter to family members and visitors. He stopped playing bass in a cover band with his brothers in pubs and clubs.

Instead, as his brothers became Christians themselves, they formed a new band that played at church services and events. In fact, we became reasonably well known in our province as news of the mini revival in our family traveled. Approximately twenty family members and their relatives came to know Jesus in a matter of months, and people wanted to know the story and hear the brothers sing.

As Dad began reading more about the power of the Holy Spirit, we moved from our parish church to a Spirit-filled church some distance away. My parents weathered a lot of criticism from our community for this. Leaving the parish church that your family had attended for generations was unheard of unless you moved towns. The Holy Spirit wasn't understood by many in our community then, yet my parents were determined to follow where God led, setting a great example for me.

I heard a lot in my home and church about a place called hell and concluded I really didn't like how it sounded. I much preferred the sound of heaven, so when I was seven or eight years old, I asked Jesus "into my heart" so I could go there when I died instead. I felt relieved and content at the time, believing He was now in my heart and I was safe from the scariness of hell I kept hearing about.

But then the doubts came. What happened on the bus when I was twelve left me with questions, challenging my understanding of God. Over time, I began wondering why He didn't appear to have my back. Couldn't God have sent help, another person to step up with me? Maybe He didn't send help because I shouldn't have spoken up. Or perhaps He wasn't in my heart after all and, therefore, was not obligated to help me? I began longing for an experience with God to know He was real and living within me.

In our youth group, which at the time had an age range of thirteen to thirty-something, if I was asked to share my testimony, I always said no. Most of the stories shared were from people saved from addictions or life in paramilitary organizations. They had a "real" story to tell, and at the time, I believed mine was insignificant in comparison.

I imagined my testimony would be so disappointing to those listening, and the doubts I had about God surely disqualified me anyway! If there was one thing small-town culture taught me, it was that people were judgmental and news travels fast. If I were honest with my story, my doubts would be on blast, and I couldn't get up there and pretend.

By far the most positive thing to come from my time in youth group was meeting my husband, Adrian. He played in a band and stole my heart long before our respective friend groups ever merged. When we eventually started dating, we both knew very quickly it was a forever thing.

While this new adventure should have been a happy time (and, truly, most of the time it was), when it emerged that some of his band members were not as happy for us as we thought, it brought a lot of confusion to my identity. It haunted me for a long time—chipping away at my confidence and self-worth.

Nonetheless, we held firm to our belief that God brought us together. As our wedding day approached, my dreams of leaving Northern Ireland became reality. Adrian spent the year before living in England, as it made sense for all the traveling he did with the band there and across Europe, so we planned to settle into our new life together there.

New members had joined the band now, leaving just one in opposition to me, but I always carried the fear my character was being assassinated behind my back. There wasn't much choice for either of us—as I wanted to be with the love of my life, and this band was his livelihood—so we pretended to get along. I leaned into my new adventure, believing it would help me outrun my fears and a growing lack of self-worth.

I kept myself busy traveling with Adrian whenever I could and working to do my part for our financial stability. I didn't have time to look at what was under the surface weighing me down. Over the years, I found more things to be busy with—ways to build my worth and identity so I could bury rising fears and insecurities.

In the back of my mind, I questioned if God could really love me unconditionally. The fun and confident version of me was great at putting on an outward show, yet on the inside, I was drying up. But the time was coming when I couldn't run away from who I was. Eventually, I needed to come up with an answer, scared or not.

Until now, I would never have dreamed I'd be brave enough to share my story, especially in a book. What I didn't understand for a long time is that my story never had to do with how many bad things or desperate circumstances I was rescued from or overcame but everything to do with my relationship with Jesus and His faithfulness.

I had no idea what I was really saying yes to when God asked us to go on a new family adventure with our children, making our home in the United States, but, thankfully, He did. It was a journey I never knew I needed. One in which He continually watered the wilderness of my heart, healing places that were parched for so long, eventually giving rise to streams so deep and strong they would last the rest of my life and overflow into my family.

It wasn't an easy journey, and the transition didn't go as smoothly for everyone as we had hoped—especially our daughters. Watching them trying to get to grips with their new lives was tough, and I doubted many times how God could have any purpose in it.

I rationalized that if He showed us how it would all turn out, it would settle my fears and worries for them, and I could live in peace. But that doesn't require faith or trust in Him, which I soon discovered were not as strong in me as I wanted to believe they were.

I'm often comfortable in the company of my thoughts. I love being with them—experiencing the thrill of questions they might pose and the possible answers they come up with as they meander around in my head—but I learned that if I entertain them too long, focused only on my circumstances without bringing God into them, those same thoughts attack me. The doubts and fears are hard to silence without the level of trust in God that only maturity of faith brings.

Oswald Chambers, in his devotional *My Utmost for His Highest*, says,

> When God gets us alone through suffering, heartbreak, temptation, disappointment, sickness, or by thwarted desires, a broken friendship, or a new friendship—when He gets us absolutely alone, and we are totally speechless, unable to ask even one question, then He begins to teach us.

That's where I found myself in this new adventure: alone. I no longer had any of the things around me that I built my worth, value, and purpose on. I had no job outside the home, standing in the community, or church community. My thoughts were no longer my friend. Yet that's where God met me, slowed down in life and alone. Emotionally exhausted and feeling like a nobody, He showed me that I was someone with value whom He loved deeply. He invited me into a new adventure: surrender.

All my life, I've battled insecurities, worrying one day I'd disappoint God or become such a burden that He'd decide I wasn't worth His time. When we encountered constant challenges in our new country, eventually, I couldn't truthfully encourage my family by saying God would work it out as we trusted Him. Deep down, I didn't know if I could trust Him. *Was He really my friend if life was this hard?*

Hope all but evaporated, and hopelessness began to engulf the atmosphere of our home, yet this adventure brought me healing, bringing Him back into the center of my life, and it has been the best adventure yet.

As I share more of this story with you, it's my desire that the streams God gave me to walk in demonstrate the depth of His love for every one of us. I pray that the value I saw in myself from His careful crafting of the details of my story brings new or fresh understanding of who He is in yours. I pray you discover Him to be more kind, faithful, long-suffering, forgiving, and trustworthy than you ever thought possible!

I hope there is faith, courage, and strength to be found in my story—to push through the hard things in life, knowing the One who values us most never leaves. May you be encouraged to invite God into your surrender—bringing streams of peace, faith, and hope into your life and home.

"Bring the whole tithe into the storehouse, that there may be food in my house. Test me in this," says the LORD Almighty, "and see if I will not throw open the floodgates of heaven and pour out so much blessing that there will not be room enough to store it."

— MALACHI 3:10

I believe God is delighted when we look for Him and follow His voice. I found Him willing to be tested, bringing about the changes I desperately needed and pouring out blessings in more abundance than I thought possible.

He is on our side, keen for us to know and nurture our relationship with Him from a place of His love and safety, not our doubts and fears. Even if our faith is hanging on by a thread or we feel we have lost it completely, it's never too late with Him.

Whatever wilderness you find yourself in, may this testimony encourage you to find the streams that lead you back to Him, the greatest stream of all.

May His name always be glorified.

CHAPTER 1

AN UNEXPECTED ADVENTURE

Years before our move to America in 2013, we had an opportunity to move there with Adrian's band, but when he played his last gig, we left all thoughts of ever moving abroad behind. It would have been his dream then, and I would have welcomed another adventure.

We agonized over what to do, eventually concluding that if God was in it, then it wouldn't be that agonizing to decide, so with peace, we closed the door, thinking it was closed for good.

We were also trying to start our family at the time, so the fact that Adrian transitioned to a job at a record label, providing regular income, supported our decision. It never occurred to us when we had our family years later that the opportunity would ever cycle back.

Funny enough, someone did say that to us when our children came along, and at the time, I completely agreed. Sometime in 2011, the opportunity came again when the record label was bought by an American company.

One evening, as my husband discussed the purchase with me —what it might mean and change—a deep sense of knowing stirred within me, followed quickly by an unexpected pang of excitement. I didn't understand it fully, but I looked at him and said something along the lines of "I think we might be going to America."

I knew he was shocked by the way he raised his eyebrows and stared at me. I interpreted this as surprise that I entertained the idea—being as I felt so settled where we were and so did our children—but it only took him a second to engage me in a conversation where we both realized very quickly that the thought had crossed both our minds.

Knowing we felt the same way, we talked about how our children might be impacted. How would they feel about leaving everything they'd ever known? Could we do that to them?

It felt agonizing in that moment to feel our own excitement at the possibility and at the same time be concerned for how it would affect our daughters (particularly our eldest, who was the more introverted of the two). In the end, we decided to leave it with God and cross that bridge if (or when) it ever looked like a reality.

A few months after our conversation, the company's president talked with my husband, floating the idea of Adrian working in their Colorado office. After some time without hearing anything more, we accepted, for a second time, that God closed the door.

As autumn 2012 came, the conversation opened again, and Adrian was given a job description to consider. We prayed earnestly and discussed it with our children. Our youngest was excited, but as we suspected, our eldest was very much resigned to the fact she didn't have much of a choice. She tried to lean into the excitement of the adventure, but I knew her heart was heavy. I hoped and prayed that if we did move, she'd soon see it was a great opportunity for her too.

As we came to give our yes, so many people remarked that at least we wouldn't need to learn a new language. This makes me smile now—if only they knew how many acronyms just in education we had to learn!

On the day we closed the door to our UK home for the final time, the sun shone. Our little seaside town always looked so inviting in the sunshine, and as friends came to say their final goodbyes, my excitement was lost in those moments. Heartbreak rose, but there was no turning back.

On August 29, 2013, we wheeled the biggest suitcases we could, filled with vacuum bags that held as many clothes as we could fit inside. Our little family of four flew out of the UK to our new God-appointed adventure in the United States. The rest of our possessions were ahead of us in a container somewhere in the Atlantic Ocean.

This was by far the riskiest thing we had ever done together as a family, but Adrian and I were confident of God's new appointment. Though I didn't realize it at the time, this was a truth I came to hold onto very tightly in the first few months of our move. It provided an anchor of assurance, centering me when I felt the seemingly unrelenting waves of life's circumstances crashing and breaking on our family's shore.

We did our due diligence. We prayed and sought counsel from our family, our closest friends, and those who had already made a move like ours across "the pond." In the decision-making and moving process, I believed God did His part of inviting and confirming, and we did ours. He saw to it that our house sold quickly in that little seaside town we'd called home for nineteen years, and we even had bank accounts and a credit card waiting for us stateside.

This was a miracle in itself, as normally with international moves, credit scores are nontransferable, even the very best scores. You have to start from the beginning, from zero, so we interpreted it as God paving our way and part of our confirmation to go.

Of course, our faith was tested at times in the process of

moving. Although our home selling quickly was a great sign we were doing the right thing, our visas didn't come as we had hoped in time for the start of the American school year. Through all the hitches, we continually held on to the words the Lord gave us from Isaiah 43:18-19. We left with them in our hearts, a springboard into the unknown.

> Forget the former things; do not dwell on the past. See, I am doing a new thing! Now it springs up; do you not perceive it? I am making a way in the wilderness and streams in the wasteland.

It never occurred to me what the wilderness might look like before the streams sprung or that there would even be a wilderness like we were soon to experience! We simply knew that we were released from the past and something new of God's design was coming.

We weren't naive enough to think it would be easy, but we were just naive enough to think we had some small idea of how it would go. The biggest decision was behind us, right? The rest we could navigate once we got there.

The first storms came almost as soon as we arrived. We may have had our bank accounts sorted ahead of the move, but no one wanted to give us a loan for a car or mortgage, and my husband was wholly averse to renting. Consequently, we spent our first few weeks living in a hotel room, getting around between a rental car and the loan of Adrian's colleague's car when they didn't need it.

We felt in limbo those first few weeks, and it was hard to continue talking up the excitement of this being an adventure because we all knew this was our new life now—not a vacation when my husband went to work and the girls attended school.

The sheer size of their new school environment and its culture in general made them homesick. Schools started an hour earlier, the classes were longer, and breaks were too short for being outdoors, which was a huge adjustment for them. It didn't help that the school year had already started, making our eldest more anxious and worried that friendships would be harder to make now that her peers already had some time to form friend groups.

That was an issue for some time for our eldest daughter. She found it hard to make new friends. Being more reserved by nature, it takes time for her to feel comfortable in new places with new people.

Every day I picked her up from school, I felt her sadness and knew she was overwhelmed, longing for what she had left behind—for what she knew and was familiar with. I told her often to give it time and that everything would work out, but my heart broke into a thousand pieces for her each day.

Our youngest daughter was more outgoing by nature and made a friend on her first day. Even though that wouldn't work out for her, it was a relief for us as parents to think that at least things were working out for one of our girls.

Little doubts started creeping into the back of my mind, asking me if I was really sure we'd done the right thing, but I pushed them aside in my assurance that this was God's path for us. However, with each doubt, the guilt hovered.

My husband continued pursuing options for a mortgage with our realtor, and after a few weeks, we had a breakthrough. We found a beautiful home near the girls' schools, which they were, in fact, excited about. Their rooms were so much larger than before, and we promised them new beds and furniture, so it was fun to shop for that together.

In the interim, before moving into our home, some friends we knew from the UK who also lived in Colorado kindly offered us their basement to live in. At the time, we thought it would be good for the girls to be in a home rather than a hotel room, but as it turned out, they felt they had less of their own space and privacy, and relationships between our children didn't work out as we hoped. For us adults, though, it was in fact a lifeline in those early days. Being able to process all the hurdles with friends was a blessing.

After a month with them, our new home was ready, and we had a delivery date for the container with all our possessions too. The day it arrived was fun—we were all excited as we opened boxes with "oohs," "aahs," and "remember this-es." Our new house started to feel like our home as our possessions began filling it, and I hoped it would help us settle faster.

The pace of life, though, caught us all by surprise. It was much busier. Kids seemed to be in practice for sports, band, or drama rehearsals every day, with games or shows on weekends. Since the school day began earlier, I wondered how much homework or sleep got done! Maybe it was just because most people understood their culture and surroundings, and we were playing catch-up.

Regardless of whether my perception was real or not, just observing it made me feel exhausted. I was in awe of what people said they packed into their day and week, especially moms. My schedule didn't look like theirs. Was I failing?

It didn't help that I disliked driving in my new city. To be fair, though, driving has always given me anxiety, but this was on a new level. Most of the intersections in Colorado were huge in comparison to what I was used to, and those left turns at intersections really made me panic!

You know, the ones where you turn left on green while cars can come straight ahead and pedestrians can cross too? It's more of a yield than a right of way, and I wasn't used to that. In all my driving experiences thus far, if my light was green, then only I was permitted to move. I feared so much getting it wrong or making a fatal mistake, and unfortunately my hesitancies were not met favorably by other drivers—they often honked at me if I didn't go when they thought I should, feeding my anxiety all the more.

Add that to sitting on the other side of the car and driving on the other side of the road! I can't tell you how many times I sat on the wrong side of the car, wondering where the steering wheel went! The new traffic systems were also a lot to take in, but (just so we can laugh together) I came up with an ingenious plan, or at least I thought so!

Anywhere I needed to go, I planned my routes to include right turns only or driving on the service roads behind shops to get to my destination. It took longer, of course, but eventually I had one or two places I was comfortable getting to, and it felt like a huge win at the time because the driving anxiety was definitely isolating.

Then, once I thought I could just about handle it, there was snow to contend with. In the UK, snowfalls were mostly few and far between—maybe a week in January or February—but now, snow came as early as October and often stayed as late as May.

We also struggled with the pace of work for my husband. His hours in the office were longer. Out-of-town travel wasn't a car journey away anymore. Traveling by plane often meant he was gone for several days. I was used to him working weekends or evenings on a project, but this seemed to be a permanent thing since moving. We all needed his steadiness, but it was difficult to find the kind of family rhythm we needed without adding pressure to his already demanding job. The acclimation for everyone was challenging.

Christmas came and went, and as we approached the new year, my husband and I thought, given the time difference in the UK, it'd be nice to FaceTime our old friends at their New Year's Eve party—afterward, we'd go to see the lights at the local zoo. Unfortunately, that turned out to be a huge mistake.

We all enjoyed the call, but as we got in the car for the zoo, the girls' moods were somber. Neither of them wanted to pose in my pictures, which left me frustrated. I just wanted some nice family pictures by the Christmas lights—was that so hard? It wasn't the happy end to the year or start of the next that I'd hoped for.

That FaceTime was both a blessing and a curse, as it served to preserve their UK friendships but reminded them of what they still lacked: friendships, familiarity, and belonging. Remarkably, and a testament to their strength of character despite their struggles, they were both doing well academically, but without that sense of acceptance and belonging that friendships bring, both were met head-on, in different ways, with anxiety and depression.

As parents, we went from tough love to crying with them and back again. I planned family road trips for the school holidays to give us something to look forward to and create some excitement in our lives, which helped but wasn't solving anything.

The sadness of the in-between wrecked me most days, and guilt continued to engage me. It was so hard to keep telling our girls things would work out with any conviction when I was having trouble believing it myself—they are not easily fooled.

When our children were smaller, parenting was often more physically demanding, but as they got older, parenting became a lot more emotionally and mentally demanding, especially in an international move. Gone were the days when the biggest hurt they faced was a fall in the playground—when hugs and a Band-Aid were enough to bring a smile back to their face, reassuring them they would be okay.

I sensed us falling into a perpetual circle: I felt bad for them, and then they felt bad for me. We tried talking about their struggles and feelings together, but somewhere within me, I knew, in those early days, they probably weren't sharing the full depth of those feelings. They were perceptive and, in their own way, they didn't want to burden us more than they had to.

None of the storms or nagging doubts broke through in those early months. I continued holding onto the understanding we were in God's will and that we probably just needed to give it more time for the streams in our wilderness to appear. Yet as the cycle continued, I began feeling weary spiritually and emotionally from my growing worries and fears. Doubts and guilt partied around the campfire that was my life. I sensed my hope evaporating in the heat of their flames.

God was becoming less audible above the noise and the chaos my current "party animals" had created. I wasn't broken yet—I was still hanging onto God the best I could—but my family and I desperately needed His intervention.

As the first few months of the new year rolled out, I knew my "just give it time" speech was wearing thin. I believed it less and less myself. How could I turn things around for my family? Just how do you administer that hug and bandage to the emotional scrapes and wounds of your older children in believable and meaningful ways—bringing back their smile and reassuring them everything is going to work out?

When the girls were little, sometimes being removed from a situation was the answer. I pondered that many, many times. What if we got this wrong and needed to go back to what we knew, to reset?

Life began to feel dry and coarse between the planned road trips, but despite my doubts, I remembered the verses from Isaiah 43 that God gave us. He was very clear in His instruction to not look back. I had to believe things would get better soon. He would water the ground, and I used this reminder to push the doubts back down.

That's why we sold our UK home. I believe God knew it would be too tempting to use it as a safety blanket to run back to. He knew I tended to run from hard things, to stop and give up when my feelings overwhelmed me.

But if running away wasn't an option, what was?

CHAPTER 2

JOURNALING THE JOURNEY

Right from the start of this adventure, God knew we'd have some pitfalls and what they'd be! Even if things looked nothing like I expected, I am so thankful for that.

It's so obvious to me now that much of my downward spiraling came about not just because of the circumstances we were in but also because I began focusing on the circumstances themselves. I couldn't see that for the longest time. I continued relying on my own strength, desperate for breakthrough.

When we get on a plane to go anywhere, the safety demonstration always states that in the event of an emergency, oxygen masks will fall from the compartment overhead. When that happens, we must put on our own mask before attending to our children or assisting others.

Reading between the lines, that tells me it's only when we are in the best possible position that we can fully help others. It's good, practical advice, and it's the best way to ensure passengers can better help one another.

I imagine it was written without any spiritual application, yet it forms the basis of my testimony in this season, the principle God wanted to use to bring me back to life. To help my family, I had to be in good health—mind, spirit, and body—but it took me a while to realize it.

At the start of our journey, God told me to journal, but it wasn't until more than a year later, when I wondered if going back to the UK was the answer, that I picked up a pen. I desperately wanted the transition for our girls to ease, and I had a growing need to find my own purpose and calling.

It's not that I had never journaled before—in fact, I tried many times over the years—but when I wouldn't write for several days or months, I was disappointed in myself over a lack of discipline. Berating myself for failing and believing that if I wasn't going to be consistent there was no point, I'd give up.

I didn't give an exact date to my first entry. I just titled it "Seeing Out 2014." It consisted of prayers for my family and a list of questions around my purpose.

Without the familiarity of my old routines and work, my days felt empty, so I pondered within the lines of the journal about my purpose, my place in Colorado, and what my calling was in this new season. I felt prompted that day to read Psalm 1.

> How well God must like you—you don't walk in the ruts of those blind-as-bats, you don't stand with the good-for-nothings, you don't take your seat among the know-it-alls. God charts the road you take. The road *they* take leads to nowhere.
>
> — PSALM 1:1, 6 MSG

It was a perfect opener for feeling seen in a new adventure, and while God didn't answer my questions in detail, He met me in that psalm with love and assurance that He was charting my path. I continued my journey in the psalms, and my next entries recorded other verses that soothed and wrapped around my aching heart alongside my hopes and prayers for my family.

Although my entries were scant at first, the idea of journaling wasn't so easy to put away as it had been in the past. It kept persisting. Despite the fact I had plenty of gaps, I didn't seem to worry about inconsistency as I did in previous attempts.

This time, it didn't seem to matter if my entries were daily or if I skipped months. The important thing was to record the journey regardless. Perhaps I kept coming back to it because, unlike my life before, there wasn't a lot else filling my days.

I wish I had seen then how the pages of my journals served as witness to God's faithfulness as I do now, but my eyes were cloudy, and His voice often felt distant. Right alongside where my anguish and despair so often met the page, though, were the beautiful reminders that He was still there.

I believe there was another reason God told me to journal. When I wrote, I heard Him best and felt the closest to Him. God wanted to set me up with a communication pathway where He could sustain me from the get-go.

As I continued in the psalms amid my overwhelming feelings and inconsistency, God continued meeting me. Though I felt my foot slipping from beneath me, His love held and supported me. Even when the anxiety felt enormous in comparison to how I saw Him then, His consolation still brought me moments of respite (Psalm 94:18-19).

Those sweet moments washed over my heart, managing to keep my worries, fears, and disappointments temporarily at bay. I may not have let them last, but they were greatly needed. God knew journaling would become a great source of water for the dryness of my soul.

The recording process gave me moments to pause, reflect, and remember that God is faithful. I was still hanging onto Him. Not every entry was filled with answers or Bible verses, but when I felt I was drowning, He used journaling to keep me from going under.

Though I was inconsistent, God was consistent—always showing up when I let Him in. I may have entertained thoughts of abandonment, doubts, and fear as I let circumstances take over, but He kept nurturing me with verses like 2 Kings 20:5.

I have heard your prayer and seen your tears; I will heal you.

When I came across this verse, those last four words, "I will heal you," challenged me. I stopped for a moment, pondering their meaning, but I eventually passed them. I didn't need healing, I reasoned to myself. Surely what I needed was for God to make the circumstances better, wave His powerful "wand," and make our children's lives happy (and, by extension, mine).

I knew we couldn't go back to normal in a new place, but I wanted to be done with the worry for our girls as they settled in and the guilt I felt as a parent for bringing them here. I was tired of our new normal. Didn't God have a better normal for us than this?

On the days I didn't have a specific word or passage from the Lord to record and ponder, I used the journal to process my feelings. It became a different lifeline then. Having a private space to express the intensity of my emotions often brought moments of clarity. It took the heat down, allowing me to feel less overwhelmed, and it brought some relief. With my husband coming to grips with his new position and emotions, I felt that helping me process all my emotions was a lot to ask of him alone. I was grateful for another space to be expressive and honest.

Looking back, I'm amazed at the dance on the pages— pouring out all my deepest feelings and disappointments and then, a few days later, seeing God cut through that noise.

But Lord, your nurturing love is tender and gentle. You are slow to get angry yet so swift to show your faithful love. You are full of abounding grace and truth.

— PSALM 86:15 TPT

My journals became my own book of psalms, my life psalms, full of questions, prayers, and despairs but also, as I began to see later, hope. I am continually overwhelmed with thankfulness and renewed awe as I read them now, considering how I felt then.

Those pages testify to my growing relationship with Jesus and His active presence in my life even though I felt far from Him at times. They bolster and boost my faith when I need it now, and they have become a great source of personal comfort and encouragement. Without them, the retelling of my story would be more focused on my feelings than on anything else.

Surprisingly, among those early journal entries are prophecies for my life and my family's. These were words of reassurance for the present and of hope for the future that could only have come from heaven because, most times, all I could see were the circumstances. Some days, it felt like they would swallow me whole. Incredibly, God kept sustaining me even when I didn't fully see or appreciate it.

Even this book is prophesied about in my journals more than once, something I didn't realize until I started reading them in preparation for writing this. That astounds me, knowing I felt it was difficult to hear Him above my rising doubts and worries at the time. It's an aspect of His faithfulness that I will never forget.

In Deuteronomy, God asked the Israelites many times to remember His faithfulness so He could continue building a deeper relationship with them and future generations. Likewise, it has become an important way for me to build my relationship with Him.

Journaling was one of the first streams God gave me for this season. Inconsistent at first, like sporadic raindrops, but enough to meet Him there to find sustenance, eventually becoming a stream flowing with faith. I discovered that if I engaged Him in that space, right as the ink was about to mark the empty page, it was where I often heard Him most clearly.

That blank page came to represent expectation, a place where I could find my breath. I'd spent so many years trying to chase God down in my head only for Him to be lost among the jumble of my thoughts and inner narrative.

In a season of upheaval and overwhelming emotions, journaling gave me a special and powerful way to access Him that I didn't know I needed, allowing me to change the outlook for our family from despair to hope.

CHAPTER 3

HESITATION

Despite pushing the thought of needing healing away, I think I knew on some level I needed to be free of my fears and doubts. I couldn't breathe freely or be of any help to my family in the current state I was in—lacking faith, fearful, worried for my children, doubting God and myself—and He was bringing me to a place of realization.

I have always struggled to have any kind of self-confidence or self-love. Back when I was a teenager, shortly after my husband and I began dating, I found out that I wasn't accepted by two of his three other bandmates. I wasn't seen as part of the "gang," which wasn't easy to handle at that age.

When Adrian and I met, the Christian rock band he played in hosted a prayer meeting on Tuesday nights. Partway through one of these meetings (which, to me, felt the same as any other), some of the band members said the room's atmosphere felt heavy. They left everyone downstairs to pray in a room upstairs for "breakthrough."

It never occurred to me that they believed I was the reason for the heaviness. I only found this out later, as one of the band members, not sharing the same feelings, was uncomfortable enough to tell me.

I was floored—knocked out emotionally by the punch and sick to my stomach by the rejection! Adrian and I didn't know how to confront it. People we confided in were angry and upset for us and, of course, reassured me I was a likeable person, but no one had practical advice. Our community didn't confront things. It held more of a "sweep it under the carpet and carry on" way of doing things. Do anything you can to avoid potential drama.

Since we didn't know how to confront them, or even if we wanted to, we opted for what we knew to do. We prayed—hoping God and time could make things better—but the seeds of confusion I felt against my moral compass even years before on the school bus were watered with more insecurity about who I was. Lies tormented me as I strove to figure out where I went wrong.

I don't know if those band members knew that we knew what really happened when they went to pray alone that night, but they were so deeply woven into our lives that not confronting them meant finding a switch for myself—pretending I didn't know and wasn't hurt.

It was hard knowing they didn't see our relationship as a good thing and couldn't share our happiness over God bringing us together. I began adopting an "I-don't-care-what-they-think" mentality when, in reality, I cared very much.

I had never faced rejection like that before. I had naively expected they'd become my friends too. I felt stupid for being duped, which stung. What hurt the most was that I genuinely liked them, so thinking I hadn't done enough for them to like me left me disappointed. I inwardly questioned my personality and wondered what modifications I should make to my character so they'd begin to like me and I could make better impressions on people in the future.

Months later, the band recorded their first album, so we all traveled to England. It was mostly a fun time, as I shopped and hung out with new friends while they recorded. However, it seemed as though those band members were determined to drive their point of my "unsuitability" home.

At our last evening of prayer together—including the producers, engineers, and our new friends—two band members began praying over me, attempting to cast out demons. I don't remember what issues they thought I had; I only recall going completely numb.

All I heard were my thoughts, particularly, "What are these new friends going to think of me?" Paralyzed, I felt I could do nothing but sit there in stunned silence until they finished, worried my new friends would no longer want to know me.

That night cut me at a deeper level, leaving me more bewildered as to how I could be with these people for so long and for them to still resent me so much. No amount of being told by others that it was only a couple of people in my life who felt this way could paper over the cracks that were appearing at the core of my beliefs.

I went back repeatedly, grappling to figure out why they felt this way. Was it how I behaved? My family is loud when together, so maybe I was too loud? Perhaps it was something I did or how I reacted to things. Maybe it was my laugh? There was an age gap between Adrian and me, so maybe they saw me as too immature. Regardless, it was a crushing devastation that, as a teenager, I wasn't equipped to handle well.

Still, neither Adrian nor I confronted it, not wanting to cause drama or risk dismantling the band, which was gaining popularity. Yet I couldn't deny the pain of the blindside gave rise to feelings of unworthiness that gained a decent foothold in my life, growing through the years, often without my knowledge. I lost parts of myself as life became about striving for acceptance.

As much as I would like to have blamed our move to Colorado for the insecurities and frustrations arising in the journey, it'd be more honest to admit those were there for a long time. I couldn't remember the last time I felt any self-love or even acknowledged myself. When I was younger, I had more energy to pretend. To combat and attempt to cover over the cracks of my identity, I built my worth through the things I did.

I was eighteen when I left home, got married, and moved to England. Traveling with the band eventually became easier when the lineup changed completely. I did that as often as I could, but it didn't exactly bring in a massive wage, so when I wasn't traveling, I concentrated on securing promotions or changing to jobs with higher pay for better financial security.

When our children came along, I went to college for the qualifications to work in preschools so I could continue earning while having the girls with me. I helped in the community by co-running a parent and baby group for new parents and later serving as a parent governor at the girls' school.

As the difficulties of settling in Colorado continued, not being busy doing things made pretending harder. The cracks were increasingly exposed. I was plagued by the thought that— even though I was never anyone special before—I was now reduced to a nobody. I had considered myself valuable and seen only based on what I did and my ability to help others with knowledge that came from those experiences.

But now, no one knew me as a mother or a friend or knew any of my experiences. Maybe none of my knowledge or advice was relevant in my new culture, and I'd have to start building my worth again.

We met a lot of people after our move initially through Adrian's work, but it didn't help that every time I met someone new, I had to answer the question, "What do you do?" Of course, I knew it was just a way of starting a conversation and getting to know us, but in the light of what my husband did—which, of course, people were so audibly interested in—it quickly became the question I dreaded most.

Each time it came up, I felt an inward dread, and before any words came from my mouth, my thoughts reminded me of how worthless I was about to make myself look. I couldn't answer that I was homeschooling or doing something I thought people found interesting or worthy. What would they think if they knew I divided up my days most weeks between picking the girls up from school and housework?

In between those moments, I begged God to make life better, and, on rare occasions, I met someone for a coffee. It appeared to me that I didn't fit in the right boxes. It felt as if no one knew what to do with my answer, or at least that's what I interpreted from the silence that often followed it. How could I expect them to when I didn't know?

Often too keen to justify my circumstances by telling them the things I used to do, I jumped in to fill those awkward silences by informing them of how I used to be the manager of a little preschool before our move. I wanted to throw my arms around anyone who asked what I did before moving because I was so grateful they gave me a chance to "redeem" myself without having to fill those awkward conversational spaces with justifications.

I felt entirely useless and as though my life history was wiped out. I couldn't yet relate personally to those verses in Isaiah 43. I didn't understand how "new" would extend to my spiritual life.

Here I was, in America, born and raised in Northern Ireland, having spent almost twenty-five years of my life in England, and I didn't feel part of any of them. I did not like it at all. I craved belonging. Not belonging at any cost but belonging as myself.

It wasn't just me; the kids experienced their own version of this and often felt misunderstood. Not playing any sports or, at the time, being involved in the arts, people didn't know where to take the conversation with them either. This often left our eldest daughter feeling as if she was falling short of a standard or expectation she wasn't aware of.

Of course, everyone meant well and was only trying to engage with them. They just didn't understand how overwhelming and traumatic settling into another culture can be, especially if you're more introverted.

I was often told as an encouragement, "Don't worry; kids are resilient. They'll be fine," but I have since read that children are perhaps more resourceful than resilient. They try to adjust to their circumstances with what they already know rather than having an innate ability to stand up to or bounce back from new circumstances. They need us to scaffold their gaps as they adjust.

Our fourteen-year-old always needed to observe life before jumping in, but once she felt safe, there was no stopping her energy or engagement. Even as a baby, we took her own toys to appointments where we knew the healthcare professionals would test things like her pincer grip because we knew she wouldn't reach out to explore any of their unfamiliar toys.

It was hard seeing her head almost always down. It reminded me of my frame as a teenager as I dealt with rejection, and my heart ached so much for her to find her people and place. It was heartbreaking knowing she couldn't see her worth or future. I was reliving the cycle that I spent my life patching over and trying to outrun.

My husband usually took the girls to school on his way to work, so he was with them most mornings unless he traveled. Selfishly, I was glad it worked this way because it meant I didn't always witness firsthand how anxiety over the school day ahead made her so physically sick that she couldn't eat.

We should honestly have bought shares in Belvita's breakfast biscuits because I bought so many of them. Just knowing she had something in her bag if she felt hungry during the school day helped soothe my heartache, as many times her lunches also came home untouched. I wished I could be at school with her, helping her navigate it and forge new relationships. She was hurting, and I felt so helpless.

Our youngest is gifted with a more confident spirit and is probably the most adventurous of us all. She, by contrast, was excited to move. She feels deeply and cares a great deal about protecting the feelings of others. She possesses a tender heart toward anyone hurting and hates injustice.

The friend she made on her first day, upon their initial introduction, told her that she wasn't looking for a new friend but, upon hearing an English accent, changed her mind. You can't fault a child for their curiosity, but the friendship, of course, didn't last long, and unfortunately that pattern repeated itself a few times, planting seeds of self-doubt deeper every time.

It was hard watching her give herself to others in the way she was created to do only to see that generosity of heart return void. I watched it cripple her after a while with confusion and sadness until it completely shut her down. I would have willingly taken her place if I could spare that tender heart and keep the bright spark in her eyes.

Day after day, I cried out to God for them to no longer be so isolated. I couldn't understand how, with continuously praying for friendships for our girls, it could prove so difficult. Watching them question their value and become more and more isolated was hard. *Surely there must be a friend or two waiting for them?*

They were supposed to be out with friends and enjoying life. I worried they wouldn't come out of this unscathed. I felt I was failing at supporting them in this transition, in what now felt like something we, as their parents, "inflicted" on them.

Despite dwindling hopes and growing doubts, I kept

repeating to them how God was still in it all—still with us—and that these school years, although tough, were actually a very short time in the grand scheme of their lives. None of this reflected who they were or how their lives would look in the future.

Though I believed that last part more than the first, I knew deep down it was the truth, but I felt like a fraud. I knew I wasn't modeling it the best I could or saying it with the conviction I should either.

I feared none of this journey would become a positive experience for us. I couldn't stand watching them fall into the cycle I was increasingly aware I needed to break out from myself. Shouting from the sidelines wasn't going to cut it. A desire for a change within me stirred. Perhaps I needed healing because my children were in the deep end, and I couldn't help them swim.

They needed to know I believed what I was telling them. Focused on Jesus, this experience would teach them a lot about what God already placed within them and how He could hold it together as they allowed Him to develop it.

Our children needed the hope and peace that trusting God brings and to know He would faithfully show up for them, but I increasingly struggled to trust God. I felt let down and disappointed in my expectations of our settling-in process.

At some point, I stopped reminding our eldest daughter of the prophecy given to her by a family friend, reassuring her God would restore her losses, because I didn't want to make what began feeling like an empty promise.

I entertained more often the thought that it was a mistake to move. Maybe God was leaving us to suffer a while for stepping out of His will. With my insecurities and warped theologies louder than ever, I couldn't communicate hope meaningfully to them. I simply wanted to fix everything, trying to do so in my own strength since God seemed to be taking so long. It was hard watching them suffer through circumstances I felt guilty and powerless about.

I didn't start out expecting others to do all the work in finding a place for our family to fit in, but my days felt solitary, and as the months stretched out, it knocked out my hope in God and projected it onto others. Staring only at our circumstances brought desperation for someone, anyone, to fix things.

Exhaustion meant that I wasn't as proactive as I probably should have been in seeking new friendships. I thought because I was the new person, it was more appropriate if invitations came to me, so I waited. Some did, of course, which I was incredibly thankful for, but, especially for the kids, friendships didn't work out as I had hoped. People had their own demanding lives, just as I once had.

On the loneliest days, I drove to my local grocery store just to see a friendly face. The staff was well-trained there to say good morning to every customer and ask about their day. Even though I knew it was a business tactic, some days I went there for that interaction because it felt good.

When I FaceTimed with my friends back in the UK, I didn't tell them the depth of my feelings or the magnitude of my disappointment. I didn't want them to think I wasn't giving this move a fair go. I didn't want them knowing the extent to which my faith was waning either.

The enemy certainly knew the trigger points to distract me with—past wounds, insecurities, and the questions in my mind that caused me to spiral. Isolation, loneliness, and exhaustion entertain all kinds of thoughts. I wondered how much God cared about how hard this was for us. Did the details of our current situation matter to Him at all?

I became so unaware that I'd placed my hope in others, especially my husband, to make our situation better. Because of it, apart from my place in my beautiful family, I completely lost myself. I wondered if I was ever capable of anything to begin with and if I was ever as strong as I thought I was.

Yet, despite all my spiraling, God continued peppering my days with Scripture to sustain me. Verses poured out over my life and into my journal in the face of what felt like the unyielding, continuous disappointment of unmet expectations.

He never expected me to make everything work out for our family on my own, and though I do fully believe in community, I also believe He didn't want me relying on others either just then. He wanted to deepen my understanding of Him and heal my insecurities. He needed to quiet my life and slow me down so I would hear Him. All my years of running from healing brought me to this place.

If it's not too irreverent to say, I imagine God sometimes facepalming and lovingly shaking His head, asking, "Why do you choose the hardest route? I have a plan and unlimited resources! Come to me for what you need; I know all the rest and refueling stops along the way."

Yet I still couldn't fully reach out. I felt ashamed of my lack of faith, and it was hard to wait and trust that His way would be good. In the muddle I was in, my first instinct was to try getting out of it myself. I was looking to grab a quick fix and carry on like I had done before, but that wasn't God's plan. He wanted me to find complete healing, and that takes time, obedience, and patience. His process included rest periods, which I had never been good at.

As my husband grappled with his new job and never-ending pace and my children tried finding their footing, I tried to carry as much responsibility for solving things as I could. After all, what else was I doing besides housework?

If I wasn't worrying and trying as hard as I could—planning family road trips or day trips, constantly coming up with fun distractions, or finding the right words to soothe our daughters' feelings—then I felt I wasn't shouldering my part. The fact that my planned distractions weren't lasting solutions was frustrating and exhausting in itself and fed the growing feelings of failure and inadequacy.

For the sake of balance, though, there were some precious wins. Our eldest daughter discovered her school district offered an online high school education program and really wanted to be enrolled in it.

At first, I wasn't keen on the idea, as, being more introverted, I didn't want her becoming completely isolated. However, in desperation for something to go her way, I started researching.

I learned that a hybrid program existed where she could do half of her classes at school and the other half online. Though she really wanted to do all her classes online, and the guilt I carried almost got me to cave, we couldn't let her give up pushing through challenges completely. We couldn't allow our guilt as parents to override our gut instincts, so this seemed like the best compromise.

Doing school this way also meant she would graduate with her brick-and-mortar high school class, not the online class. We didn't want her to regret not having the high school senior prom or graduation experience, and I was holding onto a sliver of hope that she would still find her people and enjoy these moments.

I'm thankful for that win, as she thrived in it. I'm so grateful to the Holy Spirit for His guidance in it and for her amazing class tutor who, every year, walked us through the process, working with us to ensure that online classes and in-school classes were blocked together.

However, it changed nothing I felt inside. I was still guilt-ridden and doubting God, wondering if He wouldn't fully come through. It's incredible what desperate thoughts and lies the enemy ushered into my life when I began focusing only on circumstances.

They brought a few unexpected friends and lit themselves a

campfire to sit around, reminiscing and telling all the old stories I would rather have forgotten. I was reminded of all the times I'd failed, been hurt, or felt the sting of injustice, and they became increasingly loud and repetitive. God's voice was pushed further back into the darkness of despair.

I still wasn't quite ready to invite God in to completely heal my heart or change my mindset, though. My debilitating doubts, worries, and fears still took up too much space in my life. I knew I had nowhere else but God to turn to, yet something within me hesitated.

Thankfully, God would soon prove that, just like He is just, righteous, and holy by nature, He is long-suffering. I came to love that old, hyphenated word—I heard it a lot growing up.

The *Oxford Dictionary* defines it as "having or showing patience in spite of troubles, especially those caused by other people," but its meaning is so much more potent to me than patience. How true this was of God, being long-suffering despite the trouble I was in. It stands as a word of forbearance, of being held up and cared for.

Just when I thought I'd completely failed my family—desperate for them to find peace in the transition, struggling to discern my calling, and feeling as if God was even further away from us—He knew exactly what we all needed. Thankfully, He knew me better than I even knew myself. He saw all my panic and despair, but none of it scared Him off.

He was near, leading me into a stream of rest and proving Himself long-suffering in my hesitation, waiting for me to invite Him to exchange my sorrows for joy, just as He promises in Psalm 30:11-12.

You turned my wailing into dancing; you removed my sackcloth and clothed me with joy, that my heart may sing your praises and not be silent.

CHAPTER 4

WAITING

As we began 2015, I had a strong feeling that Colorado would be similar to the first city we lived in as newlyweds. I didn't have to linger on that for very long to know what it meant.

In that first city in England, despite having some wonderful friends, I never fully settled into life there. It was a newer purpose-built city for commuters to London, and, to me, it never felt like anything was permanent.

Finding it hard to adjust to a new culture in England made me wonder if something closer to what we left behind in Northern Ireland existed. I missed walking into a store—taking a moment to chat with the checkout person without being rushed—or meeting someone's eyes in the street, acknowledging each other with a nod or a smile. I missed the warmth of those kinds of interactions, the feeling of belonging they evoked.

After six years there, God brought the right opportunity to move through a job offer to my husband at a Christian music label in a little seaside town on the English south coast. I loved it from the start. Not too big and not too small; not too busy and not too laid back. Here it was okay to acknowledge someone with a smile or chat with the checkout person in the little stores outside the busier thoroughfare, and we made it our home.

When that feeling stirred that Colorado would not be our forever place, it gave rise to the thought that maybe nothing was coming together because God didn't intend for it to be our home. Just like in that first city, we were passing through.

Sure enough, several months later, I wasn't surprised when my husband was told by his company that there were plans to relocate the whole team to Tennessee. Since he had worked in the music business for over thirty years at this point, we were in and out of Tennessee very often. We already knew some folks there, so it was welcomed news.

I had high hopes for the move. I was sure it would be better for our family, and my battle of worth and purpose could die down in the meantime. I could get busy planning, packing, and listing our home for sale, so this battle could wait until we got to our new home.

Surely there we would find our family's rhythm, our church community, and a sense of belonging. This is where we would all settle in—yes, that must be God's plan. This is where all the stress, worry, and anxiety of the last few years would die completely!

The move was planned for the following year, but as it approached, we faced a major challenge: our eldest daughter would be in her last year of high school. It had taken a long time to get some control over her anxieties. She made a few friends, and there were even plans for her to go to prom—something I know she definitely thought she would never do!

She had battled the sickness that came with her anxiety over facing school each morning for so long. It took a lot for her to muster the strength to walk in those doors every day that first year. She didn't want to brave it somewhere else for her last year, and I was concerned we might also jeopardize the progress she'd made academically. I did not want her to suffer through a repeat of that freshman year!

Unfortunately, with our girls being three years apart, waiting for our eldest to finish high school meant our youngest daughter would have her freshman year in Colorado and the remainder of high school in Tennessee. As we talked together about it, she didn't see it as a problem. Her middle school years were, on the whole for her, a better experience than high school was for her sister.

My husband was in conflict, though. He felt the pull of his job and wasn't sure he could stay as the rest of the team prepared to go. We discussed a lot of scenarios. Perhaps he and our youngest would go to Tennessee while I stayed with our eldest in Colorado until the academic year was over.

Despite the noise in my life and state of spiritual unhealthiness, I felt God lay the message of "wait" on my heart. It was always there in the sermons I listened to or whatever I read, but my husband couldn't get on the same page.

In an attempt to better tune my ear to God's voice during this time, I picked up the devotional *My Utmost for His Highest* by Oswald Chambers, which I purchased sometime in the middle of the previous year.

I'm not sure why I bought it, really. I had no intentions of being any kind of leader or pastor, but I liked how it was bound and had some vague recollection of hearing it praised in the past. Something about a new year and a new book felt like they went together.

Almost from the get-go, the message of waiting was clear, and I noted it in my journal.

> When God brings a blank space, do not fill it; WAIT.
> Never run before God's guidance. If there's doubt, WAIT.
> Don't act on impulse; WAIT for God's timing.

As the pressure mounted to decide, I couldn't ignore it. It was as if everything in me bore witness that the message was for this particular decision. Yet my husband still didn't see it quite the same.

After many coffees together, discussing and praying about it, God brought my husband to the same conclusion. I still remember the coffee shop we were in—small and cozy, cupping a great cappuccino, enjoying the moment together—when Adrian told me he agreed waiting was what we should do. I felt such a surge of relief!

His company agreed to us staying behind while the rest of his team made plans to move. I looked forward to this last school year, thankful our eldest daughter could finish her senior year and enjoy prom and graduation. I was ready to embrace all the distractions packing and planning would give me, yet it proved to be our hardest year so far.

As much as our eldest daughter picked up her life and found some joy during senior year, things fell apart for our youngest. Adrian and I sensed that it couldn't be a good thing when one evening we were called in to "chat" with her and her therapist before the appointment finished. We exchanged puzzled looks as we walked into the room, and I held my breath.

Although we knew she struggled with grades slipping and she opted to spend more and more time in her room, we did not know the full extent of it. She was walking through the loss of more friendships, and this time, depression showed up in its meanest form. It threatened to snuff out our confident, adventurous, and bright-spirited girl in a way we were unprepared for.

I still struggle today to describe how that meeting felt. The best I can do is say that my heart was so sick that my stomach followed. Yet, simultaneously, I stopped feeling, my body froze, and time seemed to suspend itself.

In my state of mind, grappling with insecurities and mental

fatigue, I would not have known where to begin to help her. My inner resources were low. I was so thankful she had a therapist to navigate this with and realized that, though our daughter wanted to tell us, she didn't have the language to describe the thoughts and feelings overwhelming her. But once the therapist broke the silence for her, we could begin walking through it.

In a tight hug, we reassured her that we would face this together. Adrian and I prayed with her and together about her, but every time we left the house, I worried about how we'd find her when we returned. In my thoughts, every hour of the day, I begged God to intervene and protect her.

Of course, we were not perfect with the listening, understanding, or advice we gave all the time, but I came to realize trying our best and being open to learning from our daughter and her professional was a good start. Showing up to be the best "you" that you can be is the only version you can be at any given time, and I discovered God can work with that!

Despite the panic and worries of walking this journey together, it also had its own kind of beauty. Sadness and disappointment existed alongside moments of joy in our deepening family connections.

With the lack of community and other things that still hadn't come together, the family road trips we planned, giving us all something to look forward to, took on a new meaning. In the middle of the chaos, they gave the opportunity to view the time spent together differently, concentrating on being present for one another. We talked, shared music, laughed, sang, and experienced new things together.

My favorite was our trip to Los Angeles. The girls put together a great soundtrack, and every time I hear one of those songs, I'm transported to the wonderful memories that still live in my heart. Those trips deepened our bonds, gave us respite, and made my heart glad.

We may have still returned to the chaos of our lives when

the trips were over, but I can't deny the gift they were amidst a difficult season that brought us closer as a family, and I will be forever thankful.

My devotional taught me that, in life, things can be contradictory to our faith, but this is where God refines us. In refinement, we learn deeply personal things—like a new aspect of God's character or a weight that comes off our shoulders—that no one can ever take from us. These precious lessons are our possessions forever.

One morning, as I started packing for our imminent move to Tennessee, *Praying Circles Around Your Children* by Mark Batterson caught my eye. Adrian and I went through it just after our move, but it had rested on the bookshelf ever since. I felt compelled in that moment to stop what I was doing and pray in our daughter's room.

I went from praying on my knees through tears to stomping around her room, declaring who she is and how heaven saw her: a precious child of God. I found a boldness to speak God's truths over fear, depression, anxiety, and anything else I could think of that was trying to press in on her.

Over her mirrors, I prayed she'd see herself as God saw her. Over her computer, I declared that she'd pause for thought before pressing any key that might open anything harmful. I opened her closet and prayed that her clothes would carry the protection of the Holy Spirit everywhere she went.

My husband was working from home that day, so I called him in as reinforcement, and we prayed until we felt the atmosphere lighten. It had been a long time since I felt the Holy Spirit move me to pray like that, with boldness and authority.

I first experienced this boldness when I was thirteen and looking for a real experience with God. It was a few years after asking Jesus into my heart when I wondered if He heard me—if He was really there. Over time, doubts that He was there crept in, and I longed for a tangible experience of Him. Being in a

Spirit-filled church, I witnessed His power in services and meetings, but I hadn't yet experienced it personally.

One evening, as I was knee-deep in sweet treats, enjoying supper after a service at a pastor's home (think traditional afternoon tea), one of the leaders asked if they could pray.

When Pastor Rosemary walked over to me, she prayed that I would have an infilling of the Holy Spirit. I can only describe the next moments as an immediate awareness of a powerful presence coming to rest on me while unpronounceable words ran simultaneously through my head.

The presence of the Holy Spirit felt mighty yet safe—something I could trust—weighty but not oppressive, and I was in awe of it. I wanted to lean into it. As I did, it seemed to move my heart and soul from the inside. My heart pounded as something powerful stirred in me. I didn't know what to do with the words in my head until I heard Rosemary tell me not to be afraid to say what I saw.

It never occurred to me to question how she knew what was in my head—I knew enough to understand that the Holy Spirit must have told her. I spoke the words as they presented themselves, each utterance leaving my mouth and entering the room, making no sense to me but holding a powerful sound.

Baptism in the Holy Spirit, my church called it, like on the day of Pentecost. I hadn't searched for it particularly, but God gave me the experience I'd asked for. He answered a young girl's question by showing up in power exactly how I needed Him, giving me something tangible—an experience I could cling to—and more than that, a precious gift.

Over the years, however, I didn't steward the boldness I received that night through the gift of tongues well. Fear, worry, and self-doubt kept knocking, creeping into my life to steal what God entrusted to me. But there is nothing like seeing your child in crisis that awakens in you—if you've laid them down—the spiritual tools you have in and through Jesus to fight with.

Despite what God may have been trying to revive in me while praying in our daughter's room, I chose to stay crushed by our circumstances. I couldn't stop the heavy blanket of guilt and disappointment, already sitting on my shoulders, from wrapping me up tightly. I again questioned if the move to America was too much for our daughters. Did it bring too many things into their lives to overcome?

As I cried in desperation to God and my husband, both reminded me the promises of Isaiah 43 were still valid and true. I clung to those again, praying them often and asking for the wilderness part to not be much longer!

As if to my rescue, my devotional discussed how obeying God often costs others in our lives too. Tears fell as I thought of the cost our girls paid to make this move. It hadn't lined up with our hopes at all. The devotional went on to explain how our loved ones are affected by our "yes" to God, but He looks after anyone pressed into the consequences of this obedience. I needed to hear that. I took hold of it, reminding myself to still believe He was looking after each one of us.

In the story of Samuel and Eli, Samuel hears his name called and thinks it's Eli calling, but Eli eventually realizes it's God calling Samuel. After Samuel speaks with God, he must decide whether to share God's revelation with Eli. In the end, he shares the message, even though it was probably hard to hear. Samuel couldn't protect Eli from God's plan; only God could do that.

It may seem to be an unusual parallel to draw from a sad story, but it spoke to me. It was gut-wrenching to watch our children wrestle with these big battles, but as much as I wondered if running back to the UK would make things better, I knew my ideas—my plans of protecting our young Elis— would fall short.

Wrestling with God, I concluded that many of the difficulties our children faced may have happened regardless of if we left the UK. Moving was not necessarily the cause but rather the exposer of the fears and anxieties they carried deep within their hearts.

Nonetheless, what I did become aware of was that there is a very real battle for our children. Whatever battles they face, as a parent, it is heartbreaking to watch. More than ever, I needed the Holy Spirit's strength, wisdom, and guidance. I couldn't do it alone.

Though we were never able to put our finger on the trigger for the depression our youngest daughter faced, I have often speculated about it. Perhaps it was the cycle of making and losing friends. Maybe it was that her processing of the move was delayed, like a kind of aftershock.

Over time, though, its aggressiveness abated, and as she came out from under it, I caught my breath again. We all began looking forward to our eldest's graduation and moving to our new state.

In mid-May, on the day the movers came to pack the truck, it snowed. I told my husband this was God's last bit of confirmation for the move. I came to dislike the snow. It was pretty at first, but when you have to function daily in it, shoveling feet of it off your driveway for more than half the year, it loses its initial appeal!

We had waited, obeyed, and weathered this season, but we were making it out of Colorado together and in one piece.

Things were going to be so different in Tennessee. The girls were going to find friends easily, living life as I expected teenagers should—with coffee shop meetups, going to movies, and attending concerts.

My husband would establish a good family and work balance, no longer spending up to half of each month there. And since we were already in and out of Tennessee so often for his work, our church community was all set up! I wholeheartedly believed that it would be easy to find our joy again.

CHAPTER 5

DESPAIR

The first few months went well in Tennessee. The weather was wonderful and reminded me of good memories from family vacations in Spain when the kids were younger.

Being closer to the music community, there were more concerts and shows to attend, which occupied our time outside of just our family, where we had lived almost exclusively for the last four years.

We took the opportunity in the transition to visit family and friends in the UK too—something I wasn't in a rush to do before, fearing that if I visited too soon I might not come back, but at this point in the journey, I was ready and excited.

I had high hopes for Tennessee, and underneath the worries and challenges of settling in Colorado, I loved the conveniences of my life in America. Houses were more affordable than where we had lived in the UK. I loved the space and privacy that gave us, rather than the more cramped space we were used to, and the convenience we had with stores, restaurants, and coffee shops.

As our eldest daughter was now driving, the lower gas prices and road tax meant we could offer her and her sister a different kind of independence, not worrying about how much it would cost to fill the tank or run an extra vehicle.

But one of my favorite things was the size of the closets compared to what I was used to in the UK, as well as the many choices of more affordable shops to fill them. Retail therapy was something that brought me respite and momentary joy, whether I was shopping for myself, the girls, or my husband or simply buying groceries. I could always lose myself there, forgetting for an hour or two whatever hard thing was in front of me at the time.

One of the biggest pieces still missing for us was a church community. It was challenging to find a church in Colorado. Initially, we didn't settle on a church home because we spent considerable time visiting places to see if they'd be a good fit, but then it became more challenging for me to dig in anywhere, knowing we would be moving to Tennessee.

When the girls struggled to find friendships, part of our tough love was sending them to the youth group of whatever church we were trying at the time, whether they liked it or not, but they didn't seem to find their people there, so eventually we gave up pushing them.

Being in and out of Nashville frequently for Adrian's job had given us the opportunity to attend a few churches ahead of our move, so we had already decided which one was for us. I was sure this wouldn't be a hurdle. My hopes were set high for instant church community as well as a better work-life balance for my husband and friendships for all of us.

However, work for my husband was even more ferociously paced than before. It was baffling how he spent our last year in Colorado here for at least a week every month, and now we saw even less of him.

By the fall of that year, we also knew that the church we thought would be our home and community wasn't working out as we hoped. Being there week after week, it was clear that the focus was on the Word more than worship, and while both are needed, we loved to worship and knew settling there would become a source of frustration.

Feeling old worries and fears from the last four years return, I struggled harder. Turning to the book of Psalms and finding Psalm 6:1-9 (MSG) summed up my feelings at this point so well.

> Please GOD, no more yelling, no more trips to the wood-shed. Treat me nice for a change; I'm so starved for affection. Can't you see I'm black-and-blue, beaten up badly in bones and soul? GOD, how long will it take for you to let up? Break in, GOD, and break up this fight; if you love me at all, get me out of here... I'm tired of this—so tired. My bed has been floating... on the flood of my tears. My mattress is soaked, soggy with tears. The sockets of my eyes are black holes; nearly blind, I squint and grope... At last GOD heard my sobs. My requests have all been granted, my prayers are answered.

I longed for those answered prayers. Where was the church community we so desperately needed and the friendships our girls needed to find? I relied on our new city to make everything better, but instead, I felt more isolated and incredibly let down.

That was the moment any hope I held onto evaporated as despairing thoughts piled on top of emotional exhaustion. I was weary from pretending everything was going to be fine—exhausted of hiding just how tough settling in was and my battered faith. I couldn't keep excitement and joy alive, trying to distract everyone from their disappointments and struggles or trying to have all the answers.

I was tired of waiting for God to help our youngest beat the depression that, although lifted some, still hovered over her life. I wasn't sure I had the strength to help our eldest daughter through the journey of finding new friends, having left hers behind a second time. I struggled to convince myself that God still cared for us; I wasn't sure I believed it—confused by why, if we were in God's will, this was so hard.

It was strange to read Scripture describing so well how I felt —knowing on some level the Holy Spirit was trying to let me know I was seen—while feeling utterly abandoned. I wasn't entertaining giving up my faith at all, but my heart hurt, physically hurt, and I had never experienced deep despair like that before.

I thought about how it went for the Israelites as they settled into the promised land, not driving out all their enemies as God instructed. They almost continuously fought battles against those enemies. I felt like I was doing the same.

Even though God was drowned out by my exhaustion and despair, which were at their loudest, on some level, I was being pulled closer to the idea of healing, understanding I had enemies to drive out of my life. I couldn't put words to the feeling, but it stirred in my soul, bubbling there, almost within grasp of my understanding.

It was tempting to wallow, close the bedroom door, pull up the covers, and wrap myself up in the pain, allowing it all the access it wanted. Some days it won.

Over the years, I heard often that children are a gift from God. I always thought I understood that well because of my experience with infertility. Having children wasn't something I took for granted, and I expressed my joy and thankfulness to God constantly for them, but in this season, the gift they were was unexpectedly different.

I may have wanted to completely give in, swallowed up by my feelings, but I knew I had to rally for my daughters. They will never know just how much of a blessing they were to me in those particularly hard days. Even though they were unaware of their impact, they helped me through.

My husband, of course, had to bear so much of my discontentment with great patience in the middle of his own battles, but I want my children to know that their strength of presence, care, and gentle concern had a powerful impact. The desire to rally for them pushed me in the best ways, exposing a flicker of inner strength when I thought I'd completely run out.

Though I still begged God to work things out for us, especially the kids, I talked to them less and less about Him actually doing it. I couldn't bear to keep getting their hopes up only to see them continue to struggle, so I thought it better to manage their expectations.

When push came to shove, I doubted if I could trust God, and feelings of despair became so loud that I stopped caring if He did anything for me so long as things came together for them.

I knew I was in spiritual trouble, and though it was from years of Christian practice rather than anything else, I continued in the psalms because I didn't know what else to do. There, at least I felt I could relate to David pouring out his deepest feelings of fear, anguish, and desperation, and it soothed me somewhat. When I read Psalm 23, the words stood out with fresh revelations and new meaning.

> Even when your path takes me through the valley of deepest darkness, *fear* will *never* conquer me, for you already have! Your *authority* is my *strength* and my *peace*. The comfort of your *love* takes away my *fear*. I'll never be lonely, for you are near. *You* become my *delicious feast* even *when* my enemies *dare to fight*. You *anoint me* with the fragrance of your Holy Spirit; you give me all I can drink of you until my heart overflows. *So, why would I fear the future?* Only goodness and tender love pursue me all the days of my life.

> — PSALM 23:4-6 TPT, EMPHASIS ADDED

It resonated differently than before. I stopped in my tracks to ponder those words, finding their relation to my life. I held a lot of fear for the present and future, but there was also fear from my past—experiences that shaped me, inviting fear and confusion into my life from an early age. I had never outrun it; I simply tried distracting myself from its wounds.

I'd never considered how God's authority over all things could provide strength or peace. Despite how He met me with the gift of tongues as a young girl, I don't think I ever felt worthy of it, especially as I hadn't stewarded it well.

Like David, all I could do was acknowledge the full weight of despair I felt to God, but unlike him, I didn't have the same trust in who God was, so I grabbed hold of this acknowledgement, hoping it would bring some kind of change.

It was hard not to feel guilty and ashamed after acknowledging how deep my despair went and how I felt disappointed by God. After years as a Christian, I should have been better at this, trusting more and praising Him in the middle of despair—not being so easily knocked down in my faith—but the unhealed, unexposed insecurities built up, stopping me from flowing into more spiritual maturity. I was lying to myself, papering over the cracks in my life. However, I wasn't saving face with God, fooling or hiding from Him in any way. He already knew it all.

My weariness and despair meant I was finally too exhausted to even hear the insecurities roar. I was utterly empty. I laid on the closet floor, soaked with tears, longing to be numb—to not feel anymore. I told the Holy Spirit I had nothing left and didn't know how much more I could bear. "God, please do something."

I felt a nudge to turn to Isaiah 43:19. Despite how I felt amid the turmoil in my heart and mind, I suddenly saw it differently.

See I am doing a new thing! Now it springs up; do you

not perceive it? I am making a way in the wilderness and streams in the wasteland.

A slow realization crept over my heart. Those verses applied to me personally, not just to our move! The wilderness of my heart needed watering. Up until now, I thought "streams" was a reference to the ways God would make smooth the paths of us settling in America. I can't say I immediately felt better, but my tears dried as the idea of healing sank in. He intended to do new things in my heart. God was using my circumstances to speak to me!

He was attempting to bring water to the wilderness, the soil of my life, so He could plant something new. He was providing the beginning of those streams through journaling and rest from my previously busy life. He provided sustenance from books, Bible studies, and sermons. But I hadn't yet given Him full authority over my life for His healing to freely flow. To become my delicious feast in times of trouble, He needed my complete surrender so His authority could become my strength and peace.

The desire for freedom from the lies, hurts, and fears that experiences ushered into my life came alive within me, including those from religious narratives keeping me guilty and bound in their unique way. I tried to find peace and purpose in our new country on my own, picking and choosing when I heard Him and carrying a weight He never asked me to. That was what exhausted me.

I reflected on how, over the years, I did a lot of self-protecting instead of letting Him be my protector! I had a vision where all those protections from my deepest hurts, fears, and disappointments were blankets. I grabbed each blanket, wrapping it around my shoulders, thinking I was cushioning myself from the next blow or making myself invisible underneath them.

It was the weight of dragging these blankets through life that made it so eventually I couldn't move. I hadn't spiritually moved forward for a long time, even before our move. His kindness was so evident toward me through this revelation. This low point brought the moment of clarity I needed to begin to contemplate giving Him the access He needed to bring peace to my life.

I had become cozy in those blankets for far too long. They were warm and familiar, comforting even. I hadn't noticed their weight until now. They'd become such a part of who I was and had shaped me. To let some of them go meant remembering how they got there, which I had never wanted to uncover.

I've heard it said that to love others well, we first must love ourselves. I didn't understand that until then. It reminded me of the airplane safety talk—that to help others, I needed to fit my mask first. It was an inkling of how God would settle things for us as a family: changes needed to take place in me before they could come about for them.

I settled so easily for the traps of the enemy, but not anymore. A resolve to move forward again and fight better spiritually for my family grew within me. It would not be like the spiritual revival I had while fighting for my daughter facing depression or the experience of the Holy Spirit I had as a child, both of which were so easily dampened. I wanted this fire to last a lifetime in the face of difficulties.

God was faithful, and as the Holy Spirit showed me where I had grabbed ahold of these blankets and why, their mystery broke down. I could let go of some easily, but others were a different story—they were painful. And some required forgiving others, which I didn't find easy.

Sometimes in the process, as their weight came off, I felt exposed and cold. Naked even. The lightness was so unfamiliar, and I wasn't used to seeing my own skin. I was tempted to pull them back around my shoulders, and I had to revisit them several times. When I did, the Israelites came to mind again, and I thought of them circling Jericho's walls for seven days before they fell (Joshua 6).

How many of them battled doubt, wondering if they could trust God in the middle of that week, but held on, continuing to march, and God proved to be faithful? I, on the other hand, was more familiar with running away and giving up.

Hesitating to welcome the release of a burden in exchange for freedom can perhaps sound a bit odd, but some of my blankets were there for so long that I didn't know who I was without them. A moment of freedom felt so foreign that I'd reach for the comfort of what I knew, frightened to learn who I could be without them.

What would my new form be—would I like it? It wasn't that I particularly liked the form I had, but I was familiar with the brokenness of it. I had to allow myself to feel in order to heal and be honest with God and myself.

I had friends over the years who'd tell me about something hard in their lives, immediately apologizing for how they felt because they knew others suffered worse things. I'd tell them not to stuff down their feelings or make comparisons because, in reality, it didn't matter if what they faced seemed big or small against what others faced.

The fact was, something came along and rocked their world as they knew it, and it deserved to be brought into God's light for healing. Yet I didn't believe that same principle applied to me.

Deep down, I didn't believe I deserved freedom. I wasn't proving to be the most faithful follower of Jesus, and I hadn't stewarded His gifts well. The enemy used circumstances to isolate and imprison me and my thoughts to attack me, and I got stuck there. God had to get me over this belief before He could do any healing in my life.

CHAPTER 6

NO COINCIDENCES

Over the following weeks, I entered a period of reflection with God like no other in my life. He began showing me how a few of the difficult times of my life had a lot more purpose than I knew.

As I lamented to God about what had still not fallen into place in Tennessee, I found myself thinking back to fourteen years prior to our move to Colorado—when Adrian and I had walked through eight years of infertility.

As I thought back, I had a vague but strong sense that God was positioning us for our move to the US long before it was presented to us. I had never thought of it like that before. I didn't have words for it immediately, but as the sense of awareness broke through, I wanted to explore it. Sitting with my journal, eventually those thoughts became words that brought greater understanding onto the page.

Toward the end of those eight years, I faced a crisis of faith. That journey began in my early twenties, and by my mid-twenties, the monthly roller coaster of hope followed by grieving had taken its toll.

As I entered my late twenties, I found it harder and harder to believe it would happen. I felt that I'd soon have to start entertaining the thought we might not have biological children. I didn't want to have to go there; the idea, to me at the time, was too painful, but hope was running out.

I got to the point where I seriously questioned if I wanted to continue with God in my life at all. Everything seemed so unfair in that season. I was weary of the rollercoaster and mourning what wasn't to be over and over again.

Others around me seemed to be growing their families with ease, and it eventually hurt to hear their joyful news and still feel happy for them. In the end, simply being around families was hard, as all I could focus on was what I might never have. Hadn't I done everything right—marriage, then kids? Wasn't God pleased with that?

I couldn't understand why this desire for family wouldn't leave. I felt tortured and prayed often, "God, if I can't have biological children, remove this desire."

Somewhere in the middle of it all, after three or four different doctors, innumerable blood tests, scans, and two laparoscopies all telling me that they couldn't see anything wrong other than some endometriosis, which was not enough to treat, I sank into hopelessness. After everything, all the doctors could suggest was buying ovulation predictor kits since tests showed my body may not have ovulated as it should each month.

I not only felt hopeless, but I was also angry. It was the same story with each doctor, just a rinse and repeat, and the years added up. It all came to a very emotional head one day as I sat in my newest GP's office.

I was alone in the waiting room, with plenty of time to ruminate on my feelings, so when I walked into her office and sat down, I barely got a "hello" out before tears of hopelessness overcame me. Any other time, I would've been embarrassed by my lack of self-control and how much snot and tears ran down my face, but not that day!

She listened with understanding and less of the usual dismissiveness. Her solution was referring me to yet another specialist, who she believed had good results if I didn't mind his brisk bedside manner. I reassured her I was not at all concerned with his manner; all I wanted was results. What I didn't know at the time was that she went down this same road. This specialist was the one who saw her through treatment and the birth of her twins.

I honestly didn't notice his bedside manner much at all because his medical approach made so much sense. On completion of his own laparoscopic investigation, he told me the same things as the others did, but unlike them, he adopted the logic of "let's get you a clean slate."

He treated the endometriosis and some other things, like fluid in the pouch of Douglas (which, to this day, I'm still not exactly sure where or what that is), sending me home with a course of strong antibiotics. His "clean slate" approach seemed logical, and a little bit of hope emerged with it.

I thought it was exactly what we needed, but after a few months with no results, hope quickly vanished again.

Our next step included a course of fertility drugs over several months and regular ultrasound scans so a further hormone-boosting injection could be administered, but I wasn't sure if I should put all this in my body. I was utterly disappointed that the "clean slate" wasn't the answer to our prayers we hoped it would have been.

I was in a quandary regarding what was right to do. *Does God want this? Am I playing God? If I do get pregnant, do any of these drugs affect the baby?*

I jumped ahead, worried that if this didn't work, what could be next? How far should we go? I was troubled trying to discern how much intervention was too much. Could I balance my desperation for a family with what God wanted? I didn't want Him to be disappointed with me because I chose something He didn't want. Being a Christian—having to consider God's wishes amid countless decisions and overwhelming feelings—felt too complicated.

There was a moment too, back when I started working, that niggled away in the back of my mind, tormenting me each time I received another negative pregnancy test. A colleague brought a Magic 8 Ball to the office one day, so everyone asked it questions. I thought there was no harm in joining in, so I asked it if I would have children.

When the answer came up as no, there was a distinct silence in the office. Despite my colleagues trying to reassure me it wasn't real, the enemy made sure I didn't forget it. I worried maybe God would let it be so because I shouldn't have consulted a Magic 8 Ball in the first place. I couldn't shake it.

With my crisis of faith bubbling inside, we were trying to decide our next steps. One Sunday morning at church, there was an unexpected altar call. I knew immediately I needed to go to the front for prayer, but I wasn't one to normally do that. Afraid to admit I had a need, I feared people would judge me. Pride and my cultural background told me I should always look like I had it together.

The Holy Spirit did not let up, though! My heart raced and my chest pounded. Fidgeting and starting to sweat, I still resisted—informing God that I would only go if the pastor and his wife were the ones to pray with me. They knew our heartache, so I wouldn't have to explain why I came forward.

Nervously, I watched the line, noting the rhythm of the prayer team. It was about every third person the pastor and his wife prayed with, so I counted to where I needed to stand, and as my husband will attest, I leaped out of my seat, almost running down the aisle.

I anxiously watched the rhythm of the prayer team as I

waited in line, relieved when it was the pastor and his wife who came to pray with me. I don't remember anything of what they said because the moment they put their hands on me and the first word left one of their mouths, I was flat on my back, lost in praise to Jesus.

I knew I was on the floor—I wasn't being held there against my will—I just didn't want to break up this incredible moment with the Holy Spirit. I wanted to be in it for as long as possible: safe, calm, seen, and resting, but most of all, fully aware of Him.

Afterward, the pastor's wife, someone I trusted as a leader and spiritual mother figure in my life, came to inquire privately about how I was feeling. I updated her with the doctor's next steps and how conflicted I felt about taking the drugs, to which she asked, "If you had a heart issue, would you take the medicine prescribed?"

It was such a simple question, yet so impactful. It was just what I needed to cut off the confusion, the continuous cycle of questions in my head that I couldn't answer.

I knew instantly that I would take the medication. I wouldn't question that the same way I questioned this. She advised not to look at this any differently—that sometimes our miracles come from medicines, and that's okay.

It felt as if I was suddenly given permission from God through her, someone I trusted with much more experience of God and life than me at the time. I came out that morning knowing how to proceed.

I wouldn't take that kind of counsel so easily from anyone, which was something I learned early on when Adrian and I began dating. It wasn't just his band members who disapproved of our relationship. I was also advised by several people who may have considered themselves spiritual advisers or mothers to me that I should walk away from our relationship.

Owing to our age difference, they believed the relationship wouldn't work. We knew, however, that it was ordained by God and supported by our families, so since then, I have always been careful that anyone I take counsel and advice from on such personal matters should earn that right.

Later that same Sunday afternoon, while on a call with my parents, I told them about my experience with the Holy Spirit that morning. Dad shared that at roughly the same time I went forward for prayer, he felt he should pray for me before getting up to preach at his church. God led him to Psalm 113:5-9.

> Who is like the LORD our God, the One who sits enthroned on high, who stoops down to look on the heavens and the earth? He raises the poor from the dust and lifts the needy from the ash heap; he seats them with princes, with the princes of his people. He settles the childless woman in her home as a happy mother of children. Praise the LORD.

Whenever I needed something powerful to settle my doubts and questions, God again provided it in Scripture and experience. Despite my confusion about if life would be easier without Him, I knew I couldn't walk away. I knew that no matter what happened, He would always be my God. I would never be tempted to walk away from Him completely again.

I thought back to those youth meetings in Northern Ireland and how I always said no to sharing my testimony, thinking it wasn't "meaty" enough to share. I had often naively asked God to give me a worthy testimony back then, but it hadn't occurred to me that to have what I considered a "worthy" testimony meant going through hard things!

Whether it was an answer to that prayer or not, here I came from a crisis of faith—a desperate desire that my prayers for a baby would be answered—and God tenderly and mercifully gave me a promise to hold onto.

I wish I would've been able to focus more on that promise of children from Psalm 113 as I waited out the next year or so before we eventually became pregnant, but I still nursed a lot of pain. I still cried to God often, shouting at Him just as much through the continuing rollercoaster of hope and disappointment, wondering when it would end and the promise would be fulfilled.

Honestly, the further away I was from the day of promise and my Holy Spirit encounter, the harder it was to focus on it rather than the pain. As time passed, it was difficult to have a promise and still wait for it. I lost sight of the kindness of God and how that promise was meant to give me strength and hope in the waiting.

I don't know if that made me stubborn or simply speaks to my shaky level of faith, but nonetheless, God took all my pain and childish tantrums, loving me anyway and never deviating from the story He wrote for me.

It was hard to feel happy about the waiting and why God wouldn't just speed up His plan, but I'm grateful for it now and how it was beginning to make more sense. He understood my humanness, and none of my actions or reactions caught Him off guard. In His goodness, He held to His plan for my life, even if I found it hard to trust His timing.

If only I had known back then and in my Tennessee despair what I know and trust now, that period of my life would have looked very different. But we know what we know when we know it, and that's okay. God still worked between the cracks of my immaturity and moments of weakness, and five months into our treatment plan, those two blue lines showed up. To say we were overjoyed is an understatement and a half!

As the due date came closer, I decided that I didn't want to do the large, local NHS hospital pre-baby classes and instead searched for places offering smaller, private groups. I wanted somewhere I felt had time for my questions so I could be as well-prepared as possible for our sweet baby, whom we had waited so long for.

The sense that God was taking me back to these events for a greater understanding of that time in my life grew stronger and stronger. I felt the significance of that class had nothing to do with baby information or being better prepared.

We met some good friends in that class; among them were the friends whose basement we lived in during our first few weeks in Colorado. I had no idea back then that, when it came time for us to move, our first place of landing in the US would be so near to them. But God was just that good—that detailed!

As well as sharing their home, they helped me with some of my early frustrations, like translating for me in the grocery store when looking for coriander (I needed to look for cilantro) or the baffling task of trying to find throw cushions online for the sofa (I should have looked for throw pillows)! Even though friendships between our children didn't grow as we had hoped, nor was it the reason we moved, it was good to know they were there in our decision-making process and those early days.

I had long since decided the purpose of that season of infertility was to establish in my heart that God would always be part of it, but on this morning, God graciously gave me much broader understanding of it.

I now understood it was for my good that He couldn't have fully shared why I was waiting those eight years. How could we do the things we were supposed to, putting down roots in that little seaside town, if we knew one day we'd leave? It would have been hard to sow into relationships or our church and community if I lived with that knowledge for the next fourteen years. I would've been like a child on a road trip continuously asking the Lord, "Are we nearly there yet?"

The evidence of the goodness and protection of God in holding back His full plan blew my mind, and I noted in my journal that, with God, there are no coincidences. My brain scrambled to catch hold of it, putting it into words. It flooded my heart and soul with an understanding of God's kindness and graciousness that I hadn't comprehended before.

I had been so angry, frustrated, and bewildered in those years, thinking maybe I was being punished, but it wasn't true. He took everything I threw at Him and never left my side. He patiently continued preparing my way, sticking to His plan, knowing that one day I'd see how waiting on Him was not punishment. It is always purposeful, timely, and full of His divine preparation.

He worked out the intricate details, making provision for our future, sustaining me in the waiting. Not only did He orchestrate our story but also that of others so we would intersect at His appointed time. I began seeing at a level I had not before. I was always seen and cared for by Him in great detail.

It made me stop to think that in our current season, just maybe all the pieces God needed to move around to answer my prayers and pleadings were not yet in place for our best outcome. He wouldn't give my family what we asked for before we, or anyone connected to our story, were ready. It simply wouldn't be His best.

The realization tilted my head more toward Him. I began looking a little higher above my despair. His revelation nudged me toward the idea I could trust Him even when I was confused or didn't understand the journey.

I knew God as many things in my life, but I still carried the fear—either consciously or subconsciously—that one of the times I needed Him, He might decide I wasn't worth it. Lies from the enemy blinded me. I always wondered if He'd tire of me, running out of patience, and because of that, I found it hard to trust Him fully.

This revelation gave me a new lens to look at our move through, and it came with a hope filter. Just like how the low point of my infertility journey brought me to the understanding that I could never walk away from Him, I wondered if the low I was experiencing now could bring about the kind of trust in Him I could never again doubt.

By a not-so-strange coincidence, the lady who staged our Colorado house when it went on the market contacted me. She was moving to Tennessee with her family and still had my number.

As we met over coffee and shared our stories, we realized we were in similar slowed-down seasons of life, needing breakthrough for our families and wondering what our purpose was.

She talked of a British teacher and author named Graham Cooke, whose teachings she listened to on YouTube, and sent me a link to a video where he explained his perspective on looking at the hard seasons of life.

It is still so profound to me to learn that, rather than allowing the circumstances we find ourselves in to consume us and begging God to change them, we can see them as an opportunity to ask God what part of Himself He wants us to know that He couldn't show or be for us before. These seasons serve as a divine opportunity to come into a deeper knowledge of Him.

I had never looked at hard times like that before. I always went through them with reluctance and spiritual resistance—relieved when they came to an end—and accepted anything I learned with more a sense of inevitability than joy. I was not onboard with the joy James 1:2-4 talks about while navigating the trials of life.

My prayers were more "God, please remove this and make it better" and questions like "When is this going to end?" than asking how He wanted to show up for me or how I could gain a deeper understanding of Him. I did not settle into that journey; I feared it.

I feared what it might expose in me—the hurts I'd buried and my feelings of unworthiness—or what God might ask of me that I was unwilling or felt unable to give. Despite the faithful hand of God in my life, trust was an issue, and I feared giving up control, which I saw as protection.

It sounds ridiculous in so many ways to trust Him in the huge decision to leave family, friends, and community to move countries yet not trust Him in the day-to-day, but here I was!

The fact that I couldn't get a handle on this meant something was missing that I needed to find. God had lovingly walked beside me even to my lowest point of despair—patiently waiting, prepared and well-equipped to bring healing and a certainty of Him that He knew I needed. I was finally longing for it.

CHAPTER 7

SURRENDER THROUGH WONDER

By now the girls were becoming more settled. We were five years into our American adventure, and all in all, it was a much longer season of upheaval and adjustment for them than I had anticipated or hoped for.

Our eldest was working, and after an anxiously terrifying start for her, she was now doing well, finding her footing at her job and navigating a few friendships among colleagues. Our youngest daughter was doing great again with grades at school, had some new friends, and regularly attended a youth group, which warmed my heart.

More little wins showed up in our lives, and I wondered if, on a subconscious level, I could let out my breath—not staying so vigilant to put out fires for the kids.

I continued with what had become a long period of reflection on my life with God, not every day but very often. My journal from that time contains a lot of musings and speculations on my past as I looked for more "no coincidence" revelations that might bring comfort, but not a lot of revelation from formal devotions or regular Bible reading. If Scripture showed up, it was what the Holy Spirit brought to mind in reflection.

Writing became the keeper of my sanity over the years, as it was the one place I found I could continue meeting God, even when I wasn't reading the Bible, a devotional, or a study. It was a safe place to vent overwhelming feelings. Even if temporary, it brought relief, and I often found a little hope, strength, or a reminder of God's faithfulness there, so I leaned into it.

A few months into these reflections, a dear friend from Northern Ireland visited Tennessee. She's one of those friends you are blessed with in life, where no matter how long it has been since you last connected, it's so easy to pick up where you left off in each other's lives. The kind of friend who never makes you feel judged and always has wisdom.

For the first time in this entire journey, I was completely honest with someone about how hard the transition was and how I was feeling. Her encouragement helped carry me through the next few months and appeared among my journal musings too, as she told me she felt this whole move was a journey of preparation.

Simultaneously, some recurring questions showed up in my journaling as I picked at what my future purpose could be. I wondered if I was ever really any good at anything. Now that we had green card status, I could work, so maybe it was time to get a job. But what kind?

I didn't have the desire to go back to working in a preschool environment, and even if I did, I was concerned I might have to significantly retrain. The policies, procedures, and expectations might be very different, and I didn't think I had the energy for that. Scribbling these thoughts down on the lined page before me, I found myself surprised after writing the question I had always avoided: *Who am I?*

Writing in this reflective season also brought an awareness of fear's depth in my life—fear of others' opinions, disappointing God, failing, and fear itself. I had a lot of baggage to shed, and I made a list of things I felt I should get better at, with seeking God first at the top.

I had not yet made any moves toward actually seeking God for healing, not entirely sure how that should look, when I received a copy of my dear friend's magazine, *Wild Goose*. Drinking a coffee one morning in my favorite big red chair, feet curled up, I picked up the magazine with my free hand, turning to read the first article.

The article was entitled "Dreaming with God," and in it, she described how she and her husband surrendered to God, trusting what He called them to even though they didn't feel qualified. I saw similarity there in how our family felt called to whatever God's "new" was for us in America, but with all the difficulties and challenges, I didn't feel well-equipped spiritually or otherwise to handle it.

Trusting God, overcoming fears, and finding my purpose circled in my head and journals for some time. Hearing how their surrender and trust in God birthed something unique for them—bigger than they dreamed—I realized that, to change my circumstances, surrender was required.

The article's closing paragraph encouraged readers to dream big with God because He had so much more for everyone. At the end, it posed a question: *What are the dreams in your heart?*

It was as if a fresh breath was breathed into me. Inspired, I turned to my journal and let my thoughts meander onto the page, writing down my dreams. Dreams for my family to find peace, joy, and fulfillment in their lives. For us to find our church community. That our daughters would find lasting friendships to strengthen and support them.

I dreamt that, even though the atmosphere of our home had slipped into hopelessness and I was discouraged, God would hold onto their hearts. I dared to write some personal dreams down too: to live with peace, find friendships, and know who I was so I could walk in my purpose.

I hadn't dreamed in a long time; I had only pleaded and begged out of desperation. The weight I carried started shaking, but even knowing what God was asking of me, I hesitated to surrender. I wondered what it looked like. If I jumped in, what would God require of me? Could I meet His expectations? Yet a strength from within and the growing desire for change finally joined together, rising above my questions.

Writing dreams for the future pulled me again far into my past. Growing up, I always dreamed of being a wife and a stay-at-home mum. I never had a burning desire to pursue a career. Back in the UK, we lived in a fairly expensive part of the country, so after our girls were born, I still needed to work part-time. I never had the opportunity to be a stay-at-home mum, but things were different after our move.

Due to the constraints of our first visa in the US, we knew I wouldn't be allowed to work at first. We asked God to take care of this so we didn't have that added pressure on top of all the other adjustments. I believe now, knowing the desire of my heart growing up, He created that season for me.

Despite the challenges we faced, I looked back more fondly on those first years in the US, remembering the many hard but also frank, funny, and sometimes hair-raising conversations I had with our girls around the breakfast bar after school, alongside all the hugs and tears. I realized they were special, and I was thankful for every one of them.

Whether my daughters agree, these will always be precious memories for me, and I am grateful to God for creating that space for us. Even in our loneliness, with so much of that time being just us together, we found a way to foster open dialogue, allowing us to share and strengthen our bond as a family. Seeing it as a unique opportunity not everyone gets, as the busyness of life steals so many moments of connection, brought closure and gratitude to that season of our lives.

It was a great way to end my time of reflection that day.

Although I didn't like how I felt, I was ready to shed it to take the journey God was preparing me for.

Turning to the next page, the title of a poem caught my eye: "A Private Audience in Wonder."

The words tugged at my emotions, calling me out. I was filling my journal pages with similar feelings, longing to trust and surrender to God, but here, they were summed up so eloquently. In that moment, I needed God to awaken my wonder. I wrote it into my journal, praying as I did.

> When I sit in expectation to meet you, I sit alone. I want your thoughts to become my thoughts. I sit waiting. Explore my mind, my soul; mend what is broken, and make come alive what needs stirring. I sit in wonder of God, who creates and rules the universe and all that is within it. And I sit alone—waiting for a private audience —this is wonder.

Each word undid me. They had been my heart's cry for months. I was waiting, exploring my mind, and only I alone could give Him access to mend what was broken. Rediscovering His awe and wonder became a stream for this dry season, another step closer to healing and spiritual restoration.

God could not have been any clearer that I needed to surrender. On the opposite page was Psalm 18:16-19 (MSG, emphasis added).

> But me he caught—reached all the way from sky to sea; he pulled me out of that ocean of *hate,* that *enemy chaos,* the void in which I was drowning. They hit me when I was down, but GOD stuck by me. He stood me up on a wide-open field; I stood there *saved—surprised to be loved!*

God had my attention. I finished off my journal entry that

day acknowledging I needed to surrender to find out who I was in Jesus and to know more of Him. Renewed wonder of Him would allow Him to finally strip away all the lies about how He designed me that had followed me since my teenage years.

I had no idea where to start the journey still, but God knew and answered me in the form of questions that popped into my thoughts, challenging why I didn't believe I was fearfully and wonderfully made. If I could believe it for others and didn't question other things like creation, why was it so hard for me to believe this for myself?

Realizing God was very good at questions, because it deeply pierced my soul, I didn't say anything audible, but I thought, "Oh boy," and braced myself. Somehow those words held power that went deep to my core. As their magnitude settled within me, they exposed something—a lie I believed—because almost immediately I knew the answer. I had never wanted to stare at it for even a second, let alone unpack it before. *I didn't feel worthy.*

Since I was seven years old, I was aware of John 3:16 (TPT).

For here is the way God loved the world—he gave His only, unique Son as a gift. So now everyone who believes in him will never perish but experience everlasting life.

It finally occurred to me that I might have never understood that enough to fully unwrap the gift of Jesus. He loved us— enough to die for us—but I always wondered if He loved me as unconditionally as everyone else. It's almost like I felt salvation and His love came to me as part of the collective "us," and because God is fair, He had to include me. I was lucky to be "in," but He was probably disappointed in me and my lack of faith.

I realized I trusted He was good with some things in life if they involved others (because they were not such a disappointment as I was), but underneath it all, I didn't think my life or dreams mattered much to God.

I was ashamed and uncomfortable admitting how unworthy I really felt, and perhaps more so that I had entertained it for so long. After being a Christian for most of my life, it was embarrassing to admit my foundations in Jesus, my basic theology, were so warped.

I sensed God wasn't exposing my unworthiness for me to feel bad or ashamed; He exposed it to bring healing. In the darkest period of this journey so far, I felt strangely safe with Him. My soul knew I needed rescue, and only He could do it. Shame had no part to play if I was to overcome the lies dragging me to the floor.

I'd always thought correction or discipline in my life came out of others' anger or fears. There wasn't one big revelation to this, but one memory came to mind. My first piano teacher used to correct my wrong notes by hitting my knuckles with a wooden ruler so hard that they stung. She always had a tight lip, a furrowed brow, and a look of anger as she administered the blows. Even though I feared that punishment every week, it didn't make me want to do better for her; it made me want to quit.

But it is clear in 1 John 4:18 (TPT) that "love never brings fear, for fear is always related to punishment. But love's perfection drives the fear of punishment far from our hearts."

The enemy had kept me in fear, stealing what God had for me from an early age. Watching my reactions, he kept me there, cowering and afraid of who I thought God was. I was blinded to who I was created to be. But unlike this broken world, love had come for me in the perfect form of Jesus. And now, my desire to surrender was flowing toward Him.

CHAPTER 8

CHERISHED

As the girls continued finding their footing in Tennessee and gaining more independence, I had plenty of time to work on surrender with God—almost like He planned it that way!

I was home alone now most days of the week, and as I so often did when I wasn't sure what to read, I went back to the psalms. It was in the quiet stillness of one of those mornings that I read Psalm 139, and its words were so beautiful.

Lord, you know everything there is to know about me. You perceive every moment of my heart and soul, and you understand my every thought before it even enters my mind. You are so intimately aware of me, Lord. You read my heart like an open book and you know all the words I'm about to speak before I even start a sentence! You know every step I will take before my journey even begins. You've gone into my future to prepare the way, and in kindness you follow behind me to spare me from the harm of my past. You have laid your hand on me!

— PSALM 139:1-5 TPT

It was the first time reading this psalm that it felt personal to me. It wasn't just nice words; this was deeply personal.

I didn't find my journal immediately to engage in some deep thinking or reflection as I normally would have. All I could do was pause, letting tears fall as the words poured over my soul like honey to the dryness of a hurting throat.

I couldn't stop sobbing, not the silent kind but the shoulder-shaking, stuttered, breath-taking kind, as I was released by the Holy Spirit into deeper understanding of how aware He was of me! It refreshed and revitalized my soul and thinking. God was speaking directly to my heart and opening my eyes to His truth. I was indeed fearfully and wonderfully made!

My hope shifted from being in me to being in Him, building on the revelations of there being no coincidences with Him. I was filled with awe and wonder yet again. He really did care deeply about protecting me and keeping me from harm. I belonged to Him. In Him was everything I searched for in my questions, musings, and reflections.

I'd love to say that was all the healing I needed, that circumstances quickly changed, we found a church, and hope was fully restored, but it was one step in the process toward all of that. It was an important piece, a blanket of light descending on my life to smother the flames that God never ignited.

I drew a line in the sand that day. It was the start of revelations I could never go back from—understandings that went so deep I knew they would be there forever. It was challenging, but at the same time, it was a fast track of spiritual growth and freedom unlike any season of my life.

Giving up the lies I believed about my worth and likability to understand I had purpose and valuable giftings—accepting I was worthy of God's love—meant reliving some painful experiences. It meant taking time with God to heal the wounds, a reminder that the timing of this season was divine because, in any other season of life I was too busy building my worth and value in my job and work in the community. Healing from some of my past wouldn't be a quick fix, and even if I had had the time before, I wouldn't have wanted to surrender them and follow His lead any earlier.

As I sat there with those verses, weeping for the longest time and letting them soothe my soul, their meaning pulled the blinders off my eyes—like the Paul-from-Saul scales that altered everything I saw. Rather than my focus being only on my circumstances, my peripheral vision was engaged.

Looking back in my journal and those from the previous years, I now saw the realness of God's love where once my focus was on the worries and fears I wrote about. So often God met me with verses from Scripture, the Holy Spirit's voice, a sermon, or something I read in a book. I felt less and less heat from the enemy's flames that, at one time, I thought might engulf me.

Seeing Him in the details of my life started adding up, and some of the light that only heaven's truth brings descended upon my heart and understanding. Colorado was not the awful place I made it to be in my mind. Yes, it was hard. It looked nothing like I thought it would. Surely, I would have loved it if it were an easier transition, but I got to love my family there. Being present for them in a way I could not before, we grew closer, and, most importantly, God never abandoned us.

God's "no coincidence" revelation and challenging question, aligning with the depth of my despair, had brought my honest answer of unworthiness. Surrender, wonder, love, and rest flowed into my life, where once insecurities raved. Slowly but surely, healing had begun, and the lies could finally be evicted.

I continued reading the psalm, blinking through tears to focus on the words, breathing deeply into my core every single word.

This is just too wonderful, deep, and incomprehensible!
Your understanding of me brings wonder and strength.
Where could I go from your Spirit? Where could I run
and hide from your face? If I go up to heaven, you're
there! If I go down to the realm of the dead, you're there
too! If I fly with wings into the shining dawn, you're
there! If I fly into the radiant sunset, you're there waiting!
Wherever I go, your hand will guide me; your strength
will empower me. It's *impossible to disappear from you or to
ask the darkness to hide me,* for your presence is everywhere, bringing light into my night. There is no such
thing as darkness with you. The night, to you, is as bright
as the day; there's no difference between the two.

— PSALM 139:6-12 TPT, EMPHASIS ADDED

These words investigated every part of doubt and despair,
every part of my current circumstances, and also past experiences where I gave the enemy the opportunity to rob me of my
God-ordained purposes.

Many years ago, in a training session for potential church
leaders, we were divided into groups to discuss and write down
what we thought our giftings were in that season of life. When
it came to sharing, there was a caveat: if you wrote down that
your gifting was being a facilitator to your spouse, it wouldn't
count. I was devastated because that's what I chose!

Maybe I was upset at the caveat because I didn't know what I
had to offer, but at the time, I thought I focused on the assignment and answered honestly. I truly believed I made a good
facilitator for my husband, so my interpretation was that it
wasn't seen as valuable.

We both worked—he at the record label, a job that often
meant he was away from home, and I as a part-time preschool
assistant at the time. With our young children's needs and

routines, I felt that holding down the fort so my husband could serve our community as a worship leader, rehearsing to be at whatever services he was needed for in addition to his job, was the one thing I could offer. I felt completely diminished that night.

Not understanding my worth to God, lies about who I was and what I could offer compounded at every opportunity. Even though it probably warped the real intent of the night, I began believing that what I had to offer the church had no real value or purpose to it, so I disengaged. For a very long time, I didn't allow myself to get involved in anything else even when I could have.

With the words of Psalm 139 stirring my heart, I jotted down some things that brought me life, things I enjoyed and had a passion for. As I did, I felt the Holy Spirit impressed on me some of the gifts I had, and for the first time, I allowed myself to believe it, letting my past disappointment go.

I realized that the things I wanted to do instinctively and with passion were the gifts God gave me! These were the things that came naturally to me that didn't always come naturally to others. I heard that was how to find your gifting, but I could never see it for myself before. I never believed anything instinctive to me was particularly valuable, so perhaps that was another reason I didn't offer any of it in that church training session.

I thought of how I enjoy looking for ways to help and support others on mission in my community, hospitality, and bringing people together. These things were instinctive to me.

I love bringing people together over dinner. I love connecting people. It gives me joy seeing those friendships grow and flourish—for them to help one another, even if it's just for one particular assignment. I feel a sense of accomplishment if a connection *I facilitated* turns into something beautiful for someone else. It gives me purpose.

My husband and I have always done that—brought people together. It's something I think we are good at as a couple. Now God wanted me to realize it had real value, and through that, I began to see some of mine. It was something He could use to bless and equip others in their mission in life and, in turn, bring me fulfillment and joy. Being a facilitator was not a cop-out at all; it has great purpose to God.

I wondered if I devalued my gifts because they weren't the traditional ones everyone talked about in church. When I found hospitality in 1 Peter 4:9 some years later, I was surprised yet so happy; it was validation, fueling me with confidence. I never saw hospitality as a gift, especially when it came to being any kind of leader, but I have come to understand that leadership is often not about a title but about leading by example from where you are.

To accomplish the Great Commission Jesus gave us in Matthew 28, it takes everyone's gifts—not just those seen on platforms. Feeding a visiting speaker so they can spiritually nourish the congregation is hugely important.

I'd love to see the perception shattered that a gift like this is on the sidelines, unimportant, or offering little value. If we are all parts of the body of Jesus, then even the baby toenail has an important function!

God's kindness and graciousness extended further in the months ahead through conversations with old friends from the UK—not so coincidentally, they kept pointing out these same revelations when we talked about our purpose. He knew me so well that He blessed me with those extra and timely confirmations.

I grasped for the first time that if He took time to create me, then, of course, it means He has a purpose for me, so the small details of my life matter as much to Him as the big ones. Psalm 139 was revealing His love as so much deeper than I ever imagined, giving me worth.

My life had purpose, and He equipped me with gifts for that. Understanding this felt overwhelmingly good, and a new depth of gratitude and thankfulness washed over me. My adoration and love for Him grew as I realized I was always in His thoughts. He never let me outrun Him.

My identity, worth, and purpose were found in Him, not in anything I tried to build. A new sense of safety and security rested over my life, and my confidence in Him grew. It felt like a reset, an opportunity to go back to the beginning. I read on that day with hunger and enthusiasm.

You formed my innermost being, shaping my delicate inside and my intricate outside, and wove them all together in my mother's womb. I thank you, God, for making me so mysteriously complex! Everything you do is marvelously breathtaking. It simply amazes me to think about it! How thoroughly you know me, Lord! You even formed every bone in my body when you created me in the secret place; carefully, skillfully you shaped me from *nothing* to *something*. You saw who you created me to be before I became me! *Before I'd ever seen the light of day*, the number of days you planned for me were already recorded in your book. Every single moment you are thinking of me! How precious and wonderful to consider that you cherish me constantly in your every thought! O God, your desires toward me are more than the grains of sand on every shore! When I awake each morning, you're still with me.

— PSALM 139:13-18 TPT, EMPHASIS ADDED

For years, the enemy had me believing I was nothing, but to God, I was something!

On our wedding day, one of the hymns we chose to sing was

"Great is Thy Faithfulness." We began our married life declaring the faithfulness of God and that His mercies were new for us every day. How could I have forgotten that?

From the revelations of Psalm 139, healing flowed as I sobbed more tears of gratitude, a stream all its own. Sitting in wonder, like in my friend's poem, with a private audience with God, peace flooded me.

He wasn't put off by the lack of faith I handled our circumstance with because, before I was crafted by Him, He knew me. Before I was born, He spent time curating my story. He designed me uniquely and with care. At the beginning of time in Genesis 1:31, even knowing humanity would turn against Him, God declared He was pleased with all His creation.

I needed His salvation, of course, because sin entered the world. I knew that. But in never fully unpacking the gift of Jesus or understanding God's love for me, the enemy stole God's divine purposes with each lie I believed.

As if the revelations of the day weren't already enough, a word from verse fourteen leaped out at me. Complex. I couldn't brush past it. I was stuck on it, pondering it over and over until I felt compelled to check the definition. I only knew it to mean complicated, therefore difficult!

It blew my mind to find that the first definition of "complex" in the Oxford Dictionary is "consisting of many different and connected parts." Next, I looked up "complicated," discovering the first definition was "consisting of many interconnecting parts or elements; intricate."

God was definitely getting my full attention because, from my understanding, intricacy has worth!

In the past, I often wondered if I was too much, too complex for people. I came to believe I might even be too complicated for God. Since that experience in my teen years with Adrian's bandmates, I had pulled back from many relationships out of self-protection. I worried that once people saw who I really was, they wouldn't like what they found, deciding to pull away anyway. For decades, fear was the driving force of my relationships, and God was exposing it.

I believe God intended this revelation to deeply hit my soul, which it really did, to further free me from the lies I believed about my worth and value. I felt my insides uncoil—a tension I didn't know I carried was released.

For the first time, I felt as though I looked into the face of my Savior to see Him smile back. It wasn't a tight, forced smile because He had to, but a wide, easy, genuine smile of love and delight. Surrender was all it took for me to feel the freedom and healing I longed for.

God delighted in me, pleased to be invited into my journey. I was cherished in His thoughts each moment of every day. There were no coincidences in my life because He already knew all the details of it; there was nothing to catch Him off guard.

I could let go of the lie that He didn't care or that one day He'd tire of me messing up and walk away. Even the parts of me that others didn't understand or know what to do with, the boxes I didn't neatly fit in, surrendered to Him and fit perfectly into His plan and purpose for my life.

With a soul at peace, I sat in that beautiful revelation for several days. I basked in it.

In those last few words of Psalm 18:19 from *Wild Goose*, a phrase had stood out: "surprised to be loved." I was indeed surprised to be loved! I had never lived out my faith with the peace that comes from understanding the depth of that love before.

The next time I picked up my journal, I noted, under what I entitled "Moments of Deep Wow," a story I heard that helped me with the impact of that morning.

When an author writes a novel, they might open a scene by saying a character woke up and went to get coffee. It seems like a simple sentence, yet the author spent time thinking about how their character should start their day. That character is so important to them and their story that they will spend time crafting even their simplest actions and interactions. It matters what the character might wear and what the journey looks like to get that coffee. The character has worth. They are worth the time and thought spent in designing and crafting them onto the pages.

That deeply resonated. It gave these profound revelations for my spiritual life extra solidification and understanding from an everyday life perspective. If an author does that for a story, how much more true is that of God, my Creator, before He crafted me?

I mattered to Him, and He showed me for the second time that there was nowhere too low for Him to rescue me. I was made for purpose and His glory. I delighted in Him more than I ever thought possible.

CHAPTER 9

FEAR

Reaching for my moment of surrender, the pressure—the weights I had carried for so long about my identity, giftings, and purpose—began to lift. I finally gave Him permission to lead my life because I now understood He knew exactly where we were going. I could trust Him in a way I never had before.

The acceptance and love from His tender revelations of Psalm 139 introduced a lightness to my life, and I wanted more. Now that I didn't have to worry so much about the girls settling in—desperately planning distractions, managing their expectations, or always trying to have the right thing to say—I had time to heal. God was making this space for me.

It wasn't just His love and acceptance that made me want more, but it was also the fact that they revealed more of the depth of His character. Feeling the weight of a lifetime of unnecessary fears and insecurities—acknowledging how exhausted I was emotionally—wasn't because He wanted to see me in pain; rather, He wanted to heal me.

It was easier to choose Him now that I held these new revelations. I wanted to continue pursuing Him in other areas of my life where I knew I needed Him and fear was on repeat. So, we delved in. I told the Holy Spirit I didn't want to be fearful anymore and waited to see where He'd take me. As He did so often before, God used the reflections I wrote in my journals to begin the process.

Upon that deeper inward examination, painful memories of times I felt hurt, rejected, or judged played in my mind. I was met with times I felt I failed or was stung by embarrassment, regret, and frustration. Times I couldn't make peace with. Times my actions let someone down, leaving me devastated.

It was challenging to relive some of those experiences, realizing I had grown so comfortable with the patterns of fear in my life—the fear of others' opinions and of failing—that kept me stagnant.

Even looking in God's mirror of self-examination, pain and shame arose from many of those situations as they came to mind. It was tempting to settle into the usual lies. *I'm too much and yet not enough. I should not try new things if I'm going to fail anyway. I should avoid being seen so I won't be judged by others.*

I recognized that these thought patterns were deeply rooted. Existing in that state for a long time, they kept me from true purpose and fulfillment.

Developing new clarity, I understood that those were all lies the enemy used to distract from my full potential. Fear had prevented me from having the impact I could have for the kingdom of heaven. Believing I had no real purpose to God or wasn't worthy enough, I feared I might mess up, so why should I try? I was shut down and blinded, sorrowful with regret for the mismanagement of my spiritual life.

Before God had uncovered any of that, though, He graciously grounded me in the truth of His love. I thought back to Adam and Eve. If God didn't love us, wasn't pleased with us, or lost the desire to walk with us, He would have been done with us once sin entered His perfect world. There would have been no plan of redemption through Jesus. The breadth and depth of love were becoming unfathomable to me.

As I continued examining those life-shaping experiences, fear, knowing it was about to lose some of its grip on my life, fought back by telling me I wouldn't be able to leave it behind. It screamed that I wasn't brave enough. Though I had been unaware how deep fear lay within me, I considered that my enemy was all too aware—perhaps believing I was a job well done by now—but God had other plans.

God continued to encourage me to look deeper than I ever dared before. Lifting the weight of fear would have been too much on my own, but now with God's truth filter on my lenses, I pressed on.

One day, as a reel of all my seemingly worst moments played in my head for probably the millionth time, the Holy Spirit dropped words like an arrow into my soul: "Learn to fail!" I wept as the words sunk in, not fully knowing why but realizing they yet again struck something deep. I asked the Holy Spirit why I was so affected.

Silence followed for a moment, but then He spoke to me in my thoughts, revealing how the fear of not being good at things had me paralyzed, keeping me from moving forward.

My perception from the culture I grew up in meant I believed I was never to speak well about my abilities or dare to think too good of myself. These things were considered prideful and boastful, and a "good" person's aim was to always stay humble. I didn't understand then that humility is a state of heart, not just what we say.

It seemed that the best way to guard your heart against pride was to only let others highlight your abilities and good qualities for you. It was more mannerly, polite, and proper this way. I believed I could not be caught even thinking I could do something well because that might lead to boasting or pride. I played everything down in my mind and with my words. My part was to humbly accept the praise of others—not by simply saying "thank you" but by saying something to deflect or negate it.

I saw so many examples of this growing up. No one accepted praise well or openly; they deflected it by saying something usually self-deprecating. The "praiser" would answer the deflection with more praise, and both parties entered a ping pong game of sorts, praise on one side and denial on the other, for an appropriate amount of time before stopping.

I copied the behavior I saw, believing I was protecting myself from becoming prideful or being perceived as boasting, so others thought well of me. It was very important in my culture to have others think well of us. We never wanted to do anything that would risk embarrassing our families.

Trying and failing, especially publicly, wasn't an option for learning and growth. If I stepped up to do something, I had better be perfect, I thought. Ironically, I think we created our own type of pride. We worked hard at staying "humble" and being perceived as "good people" to secure that good opinion from others.

I heard the phrase "self-praise is no recommendation" many times, usually in jest, yet there was an element of truth lived out in front of me. I didn't want society tut-tutting at me or pulling disapproving faces behind my back. I needed to always be approved by others to have worth or value, and often, it kept me from stepping out and moving forward.

As I really started thinking about that, I realized the pattern of playing down my abilities came with the unconscious need for someone who would counter it. I needed the approval from others—not just from one person but from several. Consequently, if no one picked up on what I was searching for, I found it hard to know what to do. I lacked confidence in myself, in what God had created within me.

I couldn't say a simple "thank you" to someone's praise or encouragement either. Over the years, of course, I saw the acceptance of praise modeled differently, meeting people who were not weighed down by this pattern; but, because I still clung to this ideal, I couldn't shake it. It shaped me.

My fear of others' opinions needed to stop controlling my actions. It was yet another thing that played a part in skewing my identity. It was time to break that pattern, trusting what God had purposed and equipped me with.

I recognized how speaking negatively over my life denied God's unique design of me, sowing distrust in Him without realizing it. Proverbs 18:21 says that our tongues are powerful enough to speak life or death, and I had not spoken very much life over myself.

For too long, my words partnered with all that was opposite to how my heavenly Father saw me. I was making the wrong decrees over my life and, by extension, my family's and my home.

The things I let shape me were mostly built on lies, and at some point, after I let them do their best work, I placed a full stop—*a period*—to my story. Fear could get to me through many avenues, be it people-pleasing, perfectionism, or some other way, cutting me off at the knees any time it pleased. Yet I was reminded that in my weakness, God is strong (2 Corinthians 12:9).

Downplaying my abilities also meant society wouldn't be disappointed if I messed up. Setting the bar low seemed like another necessary layer of self-protection from judgment. This is where "learn to fail" began to make sense. It was time to trust God's opinion of me and to lean into His purposes, trusting what He had gifted me with.

There was so much paralysis in my life. Being starved of community in this season meant I hadn't formed the kind of friendships where I felt I could repeatedly ask for affirmation.

I realized the only person I should go to was God; I was learning it's only what He spoke over my life that truly mattered. Only His words are honest and true, and His words are powerful enough to demolish the power of any others. These lightbulb moments continued breaking down tensions I didn't know I held.

Loving a good puzzle, I kept digging for more pieces. As I reflected on one or two occasions where I stepped up to do something that did not go as planned, I realized how fierce my internal condemnation could be.

When I was a young teenager, at the suggestion of some of my friends, I stepped up to play the piano as an accompaniment to the organ on a Sunday night service at church. I was curious about my ability, even though I suspected my sight-reading wasn't up to scratch. I looked at the music before stepping up, thinking I could manage, but as I sat down to play, the pace was much faster than I anticipated.

Although I did my best to keep up, embarrassment and shame over the notes I missed welled up within, overwhelming me. I desperately wanted to go back to my seat, but it would have been more embarrassing to quit in front of everyone, so I stayed the course. In my memories, I saw myself stepping up to the smiles of my friends and sitting down beside what I thought were their now less enthusiastic faces, and it haunted me.

I've learned since then that, for a lot of people, a memory like this would be no big deal, but I couldn't brush it off. Each time I remembered, it was painful. Even years later, I felt physically sick with regret and embarrassment when it came to mind.

At the time, I vowed to avoid ever feeling like that again. I knew my society didn't take kindly to saying yes to something that couldn't be executed perfectly—there was no grace for that. I bitterly regretted stepping up. People were judgy; their opinion could be harsh. I feared it greatly and turned to judging myself the fiercest of all before anyone else could.

I'm pretty sure most people don't remember that night, but I imagined they did, rolling their eyes and accusing me behind my back of being prideful and attempting self-promotion, laughing at my failure. Just the thought of being accused like that struck me at my core. But in God's tenderness toward me, I realized He is not my accuser—that was my enemy using my experiences against me so I'd be kept from my divine purpose.

Over the years, though, self-criticism and harsh self-judgment grew, ensuring I kept pressing that full stop deeper into my story. From the beginning, Satan worked hard to skew my perceptions of experiences to shut me down—keeping my voice quiet, counting on me to stay hidden, and binding me with both the need for and fear of the opinion of others.

That revelation released me tremendously from the hold these memories had. It was like I could see them for what they were; they were no longer shrouded in mystery. They couldn't hold me down any longer.

I wasn't protecting myself by thinking I couldn't do something unless it was perfectly executed. Perfectionism only brought a fear of trying and prevented me from leaning into God for purpose and affirmation, adding yet more ink to my full stop. It was a stagnating, exhausting battle—a heavy burden that God never asked me to carry—and it had to go.

The only way to be free was to live from a place where His opinions of me were the only ones that mattered, which wasn't easy, especially while trying to break the lies that were so deeply ingrained.

If I could live in His good opinion of me, I could live free above society's noise and expectations, silencing my accuser and learning to have more grace for myself, just as God had for me. I found myself wading deeper in the stream of rest He had been establishing in my life.

I determined to speak differently about myself, my family, and our journey so far. I needed to put memories like "piano gate," which now seemed so insignificant, under the authority of His truth.

I practiced responding with a simple "thank you" when I received a compliment, resisting the urge to answer with self-deprecation. I got used to accepting it rather than pushing it away, likewise acknowledging the gifts I saw in myself to God. Instead of hiding from them, I asked Him to show me where He wanted to use them.

The language in my journals toward myself also changed. I wrote about what I believed I could do more positively and about my dreams more easily because I now understood that I deserved to dream. I wrote confidently about my wins, no matter how small, focusing on the positives of the season rather than the disappointments and stretching my gaze beyond the circumstances.

I resolved to remember my past victories, to see, appreciate, and declare the ways God cared for us as a family—even if pieces still needed to come together—letting them prophesy our future. As I trusted Him more and more, I discovered the strength to let go of any opinions other than His regarding where I should be or what I should be doing at this time in my life.

While I still longed for a church community, in the stream of rest, He reshaped my heart. Alongside it came contentment for the journey I was on.

At the juncture of where my understanding of who He says I am and my confidence in who He really is met for the first time, Satan's lies abated along with the desperate need for society's approval. I already had approval in Jesus, so I didn't need to exhaust myself striving for it anywhere else. I was exactly where I was supposed to be and who I was supposed to be. I didn't have to jostle or play myself down; I simply needed to follow His lead.

It felt so good to feel the paralysis over my life breaking down. Movement, both emotionally and physically, felt easier. God wasn't thwarted by my hesitancies about surrendering to

His process, and eventually, I settled into it, realizing the fears I gathered through life had been projected onto Him. I was too unsure about Him to give the room necessary for Him to lead me, but now He was changing my internal posture from fear and confusion to love and trust.

He had indeed shown up for me during this season in a way He could not have previously. It's a testament to how much God was working in my heart, releasing fears and lies, because there was a time when I dared not to hope He could be as good as He said He is.

I wish I could say all fear was gone from my life, but I still had to work it out sometimes. Often, testimonies are of victories only after things have passed, so I want to testify to the nearness, faithfulness, and purposes of God during His healing process.

I know that, in an instant, God can break something off a person's life completely, but for me, it needed to be a journey. I needed to enter a process of learning and failing to understand that God never gives up and His opinion of me never changes.

There are times when I may have to walk out the consequences when I mess up, putting my feelings into perspective, but He has grace and patience for my humanness. There is no expectation from God to run before I can walk. Maturing in faith isn't a perfect process, but I've found a great sense of adventure in the journey of spiritual growth as I've trusted the Holy Spirit's lead.

CHAPTER 10

FORGIVENESS

That year had started out in the depths of despair, but God met me, and though I was lifting out of it, the desperation for church community increased. If only that would come together! I'd prayed for God to show us where He wanted us planted for so long that it felt like a never-ending search. I was weary and confused by the difficulty of it.

One morning, reclined in the corner chair of the bonus room upstairs, I listened to a sermon online from a local pastor on the Lord's Prayer. I knew the prayer well, but that morning, God gave me a different perspective on what it is to pray, "Thy will be done."

I had never dwelt much on that before. I got that God was sovereign over the world with a plan for humanity, but I never thought about how it applied to every detail of my life. Seeking His will for big things, especially if they were life-changing, was somehow easier than honoring His will in things I felt were smaller, like my thoughts or what I filled my time with. I hadn't grasped before that it's because He knows my past, present, and future so well that I have security in Him and can pray this confidently over my life without fear.

I used to fear that God knowing what was in my heart devalued me and made me less lovable or that knowing how I'd act or react to things in the future would cause Him to give up on me. I couldn't hide it from Him, but I didn't like that He knew the ugliest parts of me. However, with my new confidence in Him, I found security in it, experiencing peace in surrendering everything to God, trusting and resting in Him rather than in myself.

The hardest part was staying surrendered, though! Learning to stay surrendered each time I came up against something I didn't expect, something I'd rather not face, was a test. Sometimes, when my guard was down for whatever reason, things I thought I'd overcome tried sneaking back into my life, attempting to tie me up again.

Most often, that was fear. That is why learning it was okay to not be perfect was an important step in my surrender. Otherwise, it would've been like trying to journal years before—when I wasn't consistent, I'd give up.

It was easy to silence it sometimes, but for others, it was still a battle, with fear putting up its strongest fight. But now I walked from a place of acceptance, confident in Him and my identity. First John 4:4 was illuminated in a way I had never grasped: "Greater is He who is in me than he who is in the world." Fear had to bow to Him every time.

Over several days, I kept coming back to the Lord's Prayer. In particular, "forgive us our sins, as we have forgiven those who sin against us" (Matthew 6:12 NLT) stood out. I felt a prompting from the Holy Spirit to ask myself who I had not forgiven in my life, and after some hesitation, I invited Him to help me identify those who may not immediately come to mind. I wanted to give God all the burdens He never asked me to carry, so I didn't want to miss anyone. I prayed, asking for God's help to forgive.

I never expected His help to come in the way it did. I surely didn't expect that after almost thirty years I'd receive the phone call I did from my husband, striking my heart with so much fear that it sent me into a panic.

That day, my husband went to the office as usual. He was often so busy with work that whenever he had a chance to call me, I looked forward to it. I wasn't enjoying my task of washing up whatever couldn't go in the dishwasher—wondering why I didn't just buy replacements that could—when I saw his name pop up on my phone. Eager for the distraction, I dried my hands quickly and answered.

There was none of the usual "How's your day going?" where I waffled on about what I'd been up to, and I sensed he needed to get to the point of the call. The hesitation and tone of his voice betrayed any thought that this was good news.

After a brisk "Hi, how are you doing?" he simply said he had something to tell me, which, of course, set my mind racing to what it could be. Was it one of the girls? Was a family member ill?

I held my breath, bracing inwardly for impact. His words bounced about in my brain for a moment before I understood them, and then the gravity of what they might mean sank in. There was a potential that one of his original bandmates, who'd prayed that I was freed from demons, was going to take on a project for his company.

I sat motionless, but inside my body, so much activity was taking place. I couldn't speak a word, and my heart began racing until it was thundering so hard I thought my rib cage would no longer contain it! With my mouth dry and my throat tightening, I struggled to breathe.

I'd never felt anything so powerful and debilitating before. As the pain of panic surged through my whole body, an overwhelming, sickening feeling gripped me as I gasped for air in quick, shallow breaths. Someone I thought I left behind years ago was coming back into my life, and I felt threatened.

I couldn't say a lot to my husband on the phone, and thankfully I didn't have to because he understood what it meant to me. All I really remember was him saying he was sorry to be bringing me the news before the call ended.

As I hung up the phone, it felt like a million questions went through my head. I was worried my character would be under threat. Lies might be spread about me, and I'd be on the outside again, rejected before I had a chance to solidify the meaningful friendships I was beginning to make with my husband's colleagues and their spouses in Tennessee.

I knew a few people outside of that circle who wouldn't be affected, but without local church family and friends, they were the people I spent most time with at functions or company events. What if what I'd built with them was in jeopardy and fell apart?

Familiar feelings of hurt and sadness I thought I'd buried were uncovered, and with them, anger. How dare this person step back into my life and threaten it? I was taken aback at how, in an instant, I was back in my teen years. Sick and panic-stricken at the thought of going back to living a life where I didn't know what was being said behind my back, surmising it wasn't good, regurgitated itself. I couldn't return to that life.

Even though I knew we would have handled things differently this time, I sat there, desperately trying to regulate my body, telling myself I was okay, and concentrating on my breathing as I made sense of what happened. Taking deep, steady breaths, a voice in my head cut in: "How long are you going to let this have power over your life? Am I not the keeper of reputations?"

God's question again! Like an arrow of light straight to the pain in my heart, it was not asked to make the pain worse but to expose it so the light could heal the pain with His truth.

I never managed to outrun that period of my life; I just tried forgetting it. Once the band had a new lineup, I buried those feelings with great relief to move on, but in reality, I had only stuffed them down inside.

Releasing this to receive healing would be hard, yet I knew the reward would be great. Looking at a situation that had shaped me for so long required more than a mere glimpse.

When I was finally thinking clearly again, I realized I'd let unforgiveness serve as a kind of personal revenge. I hadn't wanted to forgive; I wanted to hold it over the head of my offender because I thought doing so gave me some sort of control. I liked controlling how I felt about this person who hurt me, and I nurtured feelings of dislike toward them, believing I deserved to.

The potential of facing them again revealed that I'd only papered over my wounds with grudges, anger, and a sense of injustice, which festered underneath my unforgiveness. There was no revenge being executed; it didn't affect anyone else but me.

Slowing down, I allowed God to peel back the paper stuck to those festering wounds I had wanted to avoid at all costs—not just because I didn't want to relive the pain but because I thought I'd lose my control. I believed unforgiveness wasn't affecting me, yet it was obvious now that I was incredibly weighed down by it.

Sensing God was using the encounter for my good, opening my eyes even if it hurt, told me it was no coincidence I was listening to a sermon on the Lord's Prayer days before. It was preparing my heart for the revelations to come, for His will to be done in my life, allowing me to enter the process of forgiveness.

The answer to His question was that I truly didn't want it to have any power, especially that much power, in my life any longer. I don't know why that person from the past was in the offices that day except for my good because they never came back.

Unpleasant as it was at the time, I am grateful because it showed me how the enemy could use my unforgiveness to cripple me at any point. All it took that day was a phone call. It wasn't an easy process to forgive. Just as He began lifting the weight of fearing others' opinions and learning to fail from my shoulders, along came this. But I knew now that following His will was worth the reward. I wanted to persevere to forgive and trust God to keep my reputation, knowing the freedom there would be for me on the other side.

Deeply rooted over decades, forgiving was a practice. It meant going to the Lord every time I felt my heart hardening, intentionally asking Him to help me let resentment go. It meant taking the thoughts that wanted me to remember the hurt captive instead of wrapping myself up in resentment and pain—finding Scripture to apply to them and asking the Holy Spirit to keep my heart soft.

It helped to look at the other person, trying to understand that there may have been something in their life causing them to act the way they did. This often softened my heart when I wanted to stay in hurt and resentment.

Eventually, I came to a point of realizing it was okay if that wasn't the case because I learned to let the opinions of others go, and it was unrealistic to expect to get along with everyone in an imperfect world. My job was to forgive and release so I could keep moving forward in freedom and peace.

Without God's groundwork, I believe that morning would have been profoundly more debilitating than it was, and the process of forgiveness would have been infinitely more complicated.

The opportunity to reflect on the Lord's Prayer was timely. Just as April showers bring the hope of May flowers, He watered my life with greater understanding of the care of His preparation to bring change in His perfect timing.

CHAPTER 11

PREPARATION

As our fifth year in the US progressed, my husband was given an advanced copy of Darlene Zschech's book, *The Golden Thread*, which he passed on to me.

I was excited to read it, as Darlene is a well-known worship leader around the world. Looking over the book, I knew it'd be a significant read when I saw Isaiah 43:19 staring at me from the back cover.

> See, I am doing a new thing! Now it springs up; do you not perceive it?

Before I opened to the first page, God met me with one of the verses that had been an anchor many times through our journey. Their presence on the back of the book reaffirmed His promise and care for us once again. The gracious and kind nature of God leapt at me and engulfed my heart. I opened the book, eager to find more of Darlene's story and what God might want to communicate to me through it.

Inside I read about God's golden threads of love—mercy,

grace, presence, power, goodness, and kindness—that pull through every encounter in our lives, bringing everything together for the purposes of God, as well as the giftings and passions He created within us. Even in the toughest seasons of our lives, when God seems far away, He continually speaks love over us; we just need to lean in to hear Him.

What timing! I could bear witness to this in my life—how He kept holding onto me even when I felt overwhelmed by circumstances and feelings, doubting Him. I was experiencing rest and healing in my heart through continual surrender.

I underlined so much and wrote notes on the pages as the Holy Spirit spoke to me, graciously confirming through Darlene's story that I was going in the right direction and encouraging me to keep going. I felt God's delight in my surrender and new commitment to Him.

A few chapters in, I was stopped by a section entitled "God Is In The Now." Darlene wrote, "God's promises are usually part of a process," and I thought how true that was. I didn't see at the beginning of our journey how those verses in Isaiah would be part of a process to newness in me, our family, or the atmosphere of our home.

I was reminded that there are no coincidences with God as I focused on His golden threads in my life. There was a deeper understanding that God's "new thing" for my life was to break through every barrier necessary to birth what He intended.

Affirmation and encouragement flowed from the book, bringing a beautiful calmness to my heart, until I got to the chapter "The Power of the Table." There, I felt the pang of longing.

I desired the kind of community and relationships described —where safe people and places existed to facilitate sharing even the hardest parts of our stories without fear of judgment—a community where love and encouragement flowed.

The departure from what I envisaged in Tennessee was loud and unexpected. I was so sure a church community would be easy to find, yet it wasn't at all. Although I had experienced healing and breakthroughs, loneliness still overwhelmed me.

I missed church community and the strength and stability of being planted ever since we arrived in the US, and I was becoming increasingly desperate for it.

Over the course of our first year in Tennessee, we searched, asking God to guide us to where He wanted us to be, but everywhere we went felt like it wasn't our home. My loneliness gave way to frustration; I couldn't understand why it was so hard. Much like England has a pub on every corner, Tennessee had a church on almost every corner.

Driving by them, I would think, "Surely one of those is for us." It also didn't help that I had growing concern we were not setting a good example for our daughters. Guilt again nudged in. I wondered if I was the problem.

I questioned if I was looking for something perfect that didn't exist or if God was really saying no to the places we visited. It surprised me to realize that, in a way, I was the problem. Not because there was something wrong with me, like I might have entertained before, but because my desires had changed.

The Golden Thread reminded me of the power in worshipping with community and the spiritual strength it brings. Spirit-led worship was what my young Christian life was founded on, and I missed it more than I ever had before. Years later, I heard Darlene share how worship gives us handles to hold onto God, enabling us to push through the noise of our lives, and I was ready for some spiritual handles to take hold of.

I'd become tired of the church program that didn't give the Holy Spirit any room to move, like a hymn-and-prayer-sandwich deal, but the main part, the flavor, was missing for me because there often wasn't the flexibility between services should one run over time. I wanted so much more of Him in every aspect of my life. God had changed my internal posture, and I realized my desires for what church would look like for us in this next season were different from before.

My husband and I would describe ourselves as worshippers at heart. We knew that teaching the Word was important, but worship, for us, was just as much so. Neither of us could get away from longing for a church that prioritized Spirit-led worship over production or time constraints. Not that there is anything wrong with good production, and sometimes time constraints are necessary, but we simply wanted (and felt we needed) to be somewhere where it didn't feel like these things took the center spot.

Being starved of church community gave us a completely different perspective on what it's like to be the new person on the outside too, reminding me of my expectations when I first arrived in America, waiting on the invitations to dinner or coffee to come.

I saw a glimpse of myself that warranted a heartfelt apology to God for the many times I had not extended the gift of hospitality as I should have in the past to someone who was new in my town, making the excuse that I was so wrapped up with the busyness of life.

I knew that was something I wanted to stay conscious of in the future when we were settled again. The understanding that no one should be left on the sidelines grew passionately within me too, and I wanted to be part of a church community that made hospitality and caring for one another a priority—where the "table" we created together had a welcoming seat for everyone who wanted one.

I thought about how I felt being on the outside with my husband's band members for so long, pretending to fit in, confused as to what I was doing wrong, and baffled at what I should change. It wasn't that I remembered it now with the pain it held before; it was more of a sad ache in my heart that went outward to others rather than inward to cause me harm.

I thought of the words from the song "Hosanna" by Hillsong UNITED. I sensed it was becoming my prayer: *"Lord, continue to heal my heart and break it for the things that break yours."*

To truly create a welcoming seat for anyone who wanted it and to be part of a like-minded community, I needed more compassion for others.

The God I was getting to know wasn't a differentiator of those who seek Him. There wasn't a kid's table or a cool table with Him. God, in His love and fairness, has enough capacity for all of us. Everyone is welcome to His feast, and my family not only needed a table to feast at but also people we could welcome to ours.

When I finished *The Golden Thread*, I told my husband this was the kind of church community I felt we were being prepared for—I just didn't understand it all until then.

But did that church exist? Darlene and her husband, Mark, were senior pastors of Hope Unlimited Church (HopeUC) in Australia, which only had campuses in the US that were much further west from us. It was obviously a little too far to travel to every week!

In August that same year, though, my husband had the opportunity to travel to Australia in his work capacity to attend HopeUC Australia's conference, Gathering. On the first morning, he was invited to a breakfast for leaders. As he entered the room, he saw a speaker and worship leader friend, who also lived in Tennessee, and he began sensing strongly that God was birthing something new in that room of leaders.

As the conference continued, the Holy Spirit revealed to him that his friend was going to pastor a church. He sensed a wrestle within his friend, who had received the same message from God, which they talked about together later.

When Adrian video called me (I was only a little bit envious that he did so with the Sydney Opera House as the backdrop!), smiling, he shared what he was sensing and feeling through the conference and what he believed the Holy Spirit was revealing to him.

What came next, though, was almost unbelievable. Adrian believed his friend would return to start a church in Nashville, which would become a HopeUC campus! I wanted to know all the details, but my husband is a headline person, so I had to be content with that for now. But his firm belief in this gave me hope.

It could only have been God's orchestration to put Adrian in that place at that time because he wasn't a church leader. I was overjoyed with excitement and hope but also tried my best to temper it, not wanting to get ahead of myself.

For the next several months or so, I held onto the hope of HopeUC, and my husband held assuredly to his revelation. His own process in making sense of our journey with God meant that God brought us the same desire for Holy Spirit-led worship and a welcoming, caring community at the same time. When I doubted in the waiting, he helped keep my hope alive.

Waiting during those months, I went back over my journals from the beginning, recapping the things I felt God taught me thus far and recording them afresh as I understood them now—not necessarily how they presented themselves to me at the time.

Don't look back; streams are coming.
Writing brings me close to His voice.
If in doubt, wait on the Lord.
Find your boldness of spirit again.
God looks after those pressed into your obedience to Him.
I am never abandoned.
God connects our life experiences for purpose.

You need healing for yourself and your family.
My identity is in Him.
Surrender brings rest.
I am His design, deeply loved, and I have worth to Him.
He is kind and gracious, and He can be trusted.
His opinion is the only one that matters.
It's okay to be where I am right now; waiting has purpose too.
Failing is learning.
Pushing through the pain of the process is worth the
breakthrough.
Don't give unforgiveness control.

I meditated on this list, noting how deep a season of healing and preparation it had been. God, in His goodness, watered the wilderness of my heart, and streams were beginning to flow freely.

The end of myself wasn't an easy place to come to, dark and cold at times, with fear making it hard to breathe. It was full of questions and frustration and seemed never-ending. Adapting to our new culture in the US was hard for all of us, but I sensed a new season was coming.

Although I still longed for church community as April 2019 came around, I stayed hopeful in the waiting, trusting God, and we had some wonderful family news to celebrate.

Our eldest daughter was engaged! She met her husband through her job, as it seems becoming friends with work colleagues means you also meet their friends. We were over-joyed for them, and my heart was full for my daughter, who was seeing the fulfillment of that promise given to her when she left the UK. God was restoring what she felt she lost in our move across the ocean and more.

Good news continued to come. My husband's friend, the one he bumped into in Australia, invited us to a worship night at their ministry team's office, which deeply refreshed my soul.

I sensed a community in that room among Dustin's ministry team, and I wanted to be connected to it. Afterward, I talked to a lady there who asked what was on my heart. I got about the first word out before having to stop as sobs overcame me, taking me by surprise and catching in my throat. Even though a dam broke right in front of her, I felt kindness and understanding from this stranger who wasn't judging in ways I'd experienced before. I realized I recognized it—it was just like God's. I mumbled "sorry" multiple times for being such a mess.

After I composed myself, I shared how God changed my heart. I told her my longing for a community interested in and investing in each other's stories; caring for one another's needs as they arose; encouraging and cheering each other on; and a safe place to share hard things in our lives without judgment. It came out of me with gusto and passion, surprising me somewhat. She smiled at me, replying, "I see it on you. This is your confirmation. You will walk on water."

Once again, tears came. I'm not sure why. Maybe it was God's kindness to speak confirmation through her. Maybe it was the sense of community I felt in the room or the sheer relief to find like-minded people. Perhaps it was all of them! Whatever it was, I left that night uplifted in my soul.

Soon after, my husband got a call from Dustin inviting us for dinner with him and his wife. We went over the normal kind of catch-up conversation, asking about what we were up to and how our children were doing as we perused the menu and placed our order.

At some point over the meal, Dustin said the words we longed for and hoped to hear: he would be leading a HopeUC Nashville campus. We immediately replied, "We're in." I felt such excitement and relief all at once that I barely heard the details of how it would come about, except that they hoped to launch in October.

Regularly held worship nights began, which became worship

and information nights, as we closed in on our first official Sunday. They were powerful and enlivened my soul.

Slowly but surely, as our community formed around us, it brought so much joy and strength to worship with them. My soul felt a solidarity in those worship nights that I had missed, a connection not only to God but also to others as we lifted the name of Jesus together, and it brought a new strength to my life. We had dinner together during those nights, giving us opportunities to share our stories, forming deep connections and love for one another.

Hearing the stories of others told me that we were not the only family being molded and prepared for this. It felt good to know that God was molding and preparing others too. We all came together as a people shaped by unique and differing experiences while desiring the same things.

Many of us were broken and still picking up the pieces, looking for authentic relationships, so sharing our stories bonded us quickly, and more vulnerability came as a natural progression of that, further deepening our friendships. We found strength and encouragement in being with one another, as well as so much joy amidst the healing. As we walked together, I never felt judged for my journey. I was accepted in a way I don't think I had ever felt in a group before. My spirit soared.

The October sun shone bright in the sky on our first official Sunday, and likewise, the sun shone in my heart. I welcomed new people at the door enthusiastically, hoping if they had been longing for community, they'd feel it here as I did. We filled up the room almost completely, and I worshiped in gratitude and new freedom with every fiber of my being. It felt like home to me, safe and secure.

A few months after our first service, the Holy Spirit told me to go back in my journal to the summer of 2016. It was the year before we moved to Nashville when my husband's team came ahead of him. He wanted to take the opportunity to spend several weeks with them, so Nashville became home for that time during summer break.

The Holy Spirit directed me to the notes I made from one of those Sundays. Weirdly, or not so weirdly, it was a morning that our friend and now pastor was a guest speaker.

He preached about Nehemiah rebuilding the walls of Jerusalem by putting families side-by-side and shoulder-to-shoulder, guarding the gaps as the wall was repaired. It was a beautiful picture of the strength of togetherness, one I was familiar with now as he shared it with us at church, but there was something I'd forgotten about that first time I heard it that God wanted me to see.

In my journal, I noted that Dustin used the significance of families playing their part to describe his desire to see a church that emulated that. For church to be a place where people could come to be encouraged and built up, not just as individuals but as whole families. A body of people in pursuit of Jesus, who became a family of families willing to meet the needs of others and set a place at the table for everyone. But it was the last sentence I wrote that I believed God wanted me to remember.

I finished that entry almost three years before, stating that this was the kind of church we needed as a family, one I would be ready to throw my all into. Our pastor had no idea he was prophesying that day, and I had no idea God was telling me ahead of time this is what we were being prepared for.

That trip to Australia my husband took was a beautiful gift from God, where He signaled to us that He saw our hearts, heard our prayers, and that community was being prepared. I was lost in fresh wonder at God, full of yet more thankfulness and awe of how aware of our needs He always had been.

Every detail of our lives mattered to Him. I might have missed a lot of His signposts along the way, but it's further testament to His faithful and loving character that He never gave up on me. Despite knowing I'd miss or dismiss them, He gave them anyway—even caring enough to take me back to them just so I could be assured yet again of the depth of His care.

I may not have been walking on water exactly, but the streams of faith, love, and trust were filling up.

CHAPTER 12

REVIVED

The month before the official launch of our Nashville church, I had the opportunity to attend HopeUC's conference, Gathering, for the American churches in Los Angeles, California.

I almost didn't make it because I was suffering from terrible dental pain. I had dental surgery and was given some heavy pain medications until everything settled. The medicine kept the pain at bay, but it wasn't completely gone, so, after several days, I was concerned it might not settle at all.

We prayed that it would subside, but as we got closer to the trip, I prepared my husband that I probably couldn't go. I wanted to stay close to my dentist in case it got worse. I'd had some not-so-great experiences in Colorado finding a dentist, so I felt blessed to find the one I had in Tennessee. I didn't want anyone else near my pain.

Adrian felt so sure I was supposed to be there, and I really wanted to go. I think we both sensed it was significant in some way, not just because I knew Darlene would be there (and I wanted to hear from her), but also because our new pastors were being prayed for and commissioned into their new roles, so many of our new friends would be there.

I was in a total quandary as to what to do, going back and forth constantly in my mind. Forty-eight hours before the event, I told him to confirm my flight.

What changed my mind was probably a combination of a few things. The fear of missing out, for sure, and the sense I had in my spirit that I should go were part of it, but it was also because I knew it was unlike my husband to be so persistent. Over the years, I learned to trust that persistence, as he was usually right. I decided in the end I would press on, entrusting the trip to the Lord and pain meds!

I looked forward to the first worship celebration; it was joyous and powerful from the get-go. The presence of God was so tangible in the room, and as our voices soared to the heavens, I felt carried along and strengthened by the sound.

For the first few songs, I pressed in with my worship, eager for God to know how grateful and thankful my heart was—how much adoration I had for Him—but I became increasingly aware of the heartfelt worship coming from the lady behind me.

I kept turning back to my worship, but I couldn't focus. Something about it resonated; it kept tugging at my heart. It had nothing to do with the words she spoke—I don't remember them—but everything to do with a desperation I recognized from deep within when you've come to the end of yourself and are crying out for help.

She wept, and I sensed it was out of a deep place in her soul. I recognized it, and it continued to pull me in. As the compassion in my heart for her stirred, I battled if I should pray with her. I didn't know the other HopeUC churches well at the time, and since this wasn't my church, I wasn't sure if I could. Would she welcome me breaking into such a personal moment? As thoughts swirled around, the Holy Spirit interrupted them: "Tell her I see her."

I wish I could say that my new place of confidence in God meant I was full of boldness in everything, but I can't. I wrestled! I'd never spoken to a stranger, carrying God's message to them like that before. I was cultivating God's voice in my life through my journals, but this felt different. I wondered if it was really God. Maybe it was just me because I was moved by her cry. Unsure, I couldn't deliver the message.

Adrian and I drove back to our hotel and met with a couple of friends staying there, but the whole time we talked, I thought about that lady—what I felt the Holy Spirit wanted me to tell her—and was annoyed that I couldn't do it.

Back at our hotel room, I told Adrian the story and how I felt. I thought we should pray God would send someone to do what I couldn't. I didn't want my paralysis in the moment to rob her of the renewed hope and strength that knowing God saw her would bring to her life. I understood the profound comfort of knowing God was beside you in the depths of despair, and I wanted to be sure she had that.

It's not that I believed God would let her miss out on the message or comfort He had for her, but I felt it was important to cover her in prayer, acknowledging that I knew I missed the opportunity and was sorry. Fear swirled again in this uncharted area of my life. Adrian and I prayed God would send someone else with the message, and I asked that He wouldn't let fear have the upper hand in a new area of my spiritual life He might want to develop.

The following day, I scoured the crowd as we walked into the morning worship service, but I didn't see her. I was disappointed, though I don't know what I would have done if I had seen her. I shrugged it off, thinking it was unlikely I'd see her anyway among so many attendees, and after all, God was going to send someone else.

Resigned to the fact that I probably wouldn't see her again, I eventually stopped thinking about her. Coming out of a breakout session later, I wondered where to meet with Adrian since we weren't in the same session. As we filed out into the foyer, I happened to look to my left, scanning the crowd for my husband, and found myself shoulder to shoulder with that very lady!

As far as I knew, we were not in the same breakout group, but here we were, side by side. I was brought up short at first. Completely taken aback, I momentarily glanced back to the floor, but as we were taken along by the crowd entering the foyer, we stayed close together. The Holy Spirit broke into my thoughts: "I'm giving you another opportunity."

Just like that day in church years before, when I propelled out of my seat to obey the altar call for prayer, I felt the same pounding in my chest and a feeling that I couldn't, or didn't want to, ignore. I understood this was another opportunity to be God's messenger, and I couldn't miss it.

I couldn't hesitate a moment more, so I touched her shoulder and said something like, "God wants you to know He sees you." She nodded back in acknowledgment, and both of our eyes filled with tears.

It felt like we shared a deeply emotional and spiritual moment, albeit fleeting—understanding God in different but very personal ways. Each of us received something from God for our lives without more words passing between us. It was a momentary connection only the Holy Spirit could make, and then we went our separate ways.

During the last service of Gathering, just before worship began, one of the senior pastors approached Adrian and me at our seats, asking us to sit in the front row instead. Not being the front row's biggest fan, I fought hard against his persistence, but he remained adamant, and I quickly realized that there were only so many times I could politely decline, so off we went to the front row to fill his and his wife's seats.

I felt self-conscious the whole time, but during the altar call at the end of service, I looked up at the line that formed in front of us. Of all the places that same lady could have stood, she was right in front of me! *What are the chances?*

The graciousness of God and His attention to detail yet again overwhelmed me; it still brings me to tears. He didn't have to go that extra mile for me, but He wanted to. If there was any bit of doubt left that God's love wasn't vast or He wasn't in the details of my life, there couldn't be any longer.

When the prayer team came to pray with her, I had the privilege of reaching out with others around me to catch her as she fell under the power of the Holy Spirit's work, much like I did in my church all those years before. I felt the Holy Spirit squash my initial doubts, confirming that I had absolutely heard His message for this lady.

Even though I wouldn't always get to see what He was doing in someone's life beyond my obedience to act as He asked, I celebrated the win of recognizing the sound of His voice for someone else. I believe He graciously allowed me to see what He was doing in this lady's life to develop confidence and boldness within me for the future—in the times I needed to simply obey without full understanding.

The whole experience was a gift. It's precious and humbling to be placed, even for a moment, in someone else's life to catch a glimpse of the magnitude of the Holy Spirit's beautiful work in them. I was in such awe that God chose me.

Yet again, there was no coincidence with God. Everything I encountered was for His purpose and glory; I simply had to lean into my part. I realized how much fullness of life and purpose could be found in those moments. Not only was He proving I could trust Him, but also that He trusted me. It was humbling, but I found such value in it.

God had guided me to Los Angeles to graciously scoop me up into a wonderful encounter to give me a newfound confidence in recognizing the Holy Spirit's voice. Gathering revived more of my dry spiritual bones, and I left with a fresh new boldness flowing in my spirit. Now it was time to use it.

CHAPTER 13

WHAT ABOUT MY FAMILY?

Overwhelmed with gratitude to God, I spent the plane ride home reflecting not only on the conference but also on the streams God was establishing in my life, realizing that each time I stepped into one, it always led me closer to Him.

I was trusting Him in ways and walking in freedoms I had not known before. My shoulders felt lighter; there was air to breathe, and it nourished my spirit. *But what about my family?*

Our eldest daughter was planning her wedding for April the following year. She continued to work her job at a local coffee shop, a miracle in itself and something she thought she'd never do. Just as we had arrived in Tennessee, a friend launched a new business, coaching young people in their strengths.

Sensing God's perfect timing, we wasted no time in employing her since our daughter didn't want to attend college. We hoped it would help her settle in better and give her confidence and direction for finding a job.

At first, when the idea she'd thrive working in a coffee shop environment was suggested, our daughter was not interested. She wanted something less visible, but through her coach, God worked in her heart, and she eventually submitted an application to a local coffee shop.

She was hired on the spot by a wonderful manager who saw her potential despite the anxiety, and sure enough, she thrived, going on to train staff, hold a shift lead position, and, probably most important to her, meet her husband.

Our youngest daughter was making it through high school the best she could. Friendships were fickle, as they often are at that age. They came and went, but she had one constant, giving us hope. She had big decisions to make that were quickly approaching. It was time to decide whether to go to college or not, and if so, where and what to study.

By far the class she enjoyed the most was film and broadcasting. She was making good grades, but we sensed that underlying sadness was still following her in everything she did. We continued to pray, keeping our communication lines open, and she kept up regular meetings with a counselor.

I was disappointed that she still wasn't thriving, and even though our eldest daughter was entering an exciting time in life, anxiety—still a battle—ramped up. I felt they were both limping along with the weights they carried. The joy in life I felt they should have wasn't as full as it could be. I wanted my family to find the depth of worth that I found. I wanted us all to experience a life overflowing with joy and peace.

Being confused about who I was had left me cautious in so many friendships through the years, never able to settle into them with confidence. I always waited for the other shoe to drop, desperate to make a good impression, plagued by the question of if I were truly myself, would I really be liked and accepted?

I didn't want our daughters to continue facing this. I wanted them to know their acceptance was in God—that their value had nothing to do with their skills, career, or what they did (or didn't) do—so they could walk in the peace of His truth, unhindered by lies and confusion.

While discovering and learning to accept my design, I discovered that I loved celebrating others' wins and was comfortable crying with them in their pain. I want to be honest and vulnerable with someone, hearing their joys and sorrows with equal attention—a part of me so often shut down in the past.

Until finding my HopeUC community, I was vulnerable with very few people. That kind of vulnerability was unwelcome in my formative years. I didn't have life experiences to share then, but I sought people to share my hurts and pain with. I often felt the discomfort of those conversations by the facial expression of the other person—a forced smile that didn't feel warm to ward off the awkwardness felt. They hesitated to answer directly, instead changing the subject. Yet I couldn't deny it was inherent to me.

I didn't have the language for all of that then, but I gleaned that vulnerability was unwelcome. My culture considered it oversharing, something we apparently shouldn't do. Perhaps my "oversharing" didn't preserve the British stiff upper lip? Maybe it went back to not wanting to invite the judgment of others, or perhaps it was pride in not letting our community know we were imperfect.

Regardless of the reason, a conflict of what was integral to me against what society deemed proper was silencing. I was created to wear my heart on my sleeve, sharing the experiences I went through and what I wrestled with, in the hope others found strength and comfort from it. Confused by who I was and lacking confidence in God, I could never lay the person He created me to be at His feet, letting Him use me however He needed.

HopeUC showed me how much encouragement there was to be found in the vulnerability of telling our stories, and I believed my Los Angeles experience confirmed God wanted to use me to encourage others. Now that I felt I could be more of my true self, I was liberated from the heavy shackles I dragged around most of my life, released more into my purpose.

Too long was I in a constant struggle between who I was created to be and the rules of the unseen "they," blinding me to the fact that sharing our stories is a powerful gift. Carrying from my teens a lie that my story didn't matter, believing I had nothing interesting or "meaty" to offer, the truth was buried. Stories matter because they testify to the faithfulness of God and prophesy hope to the lives of others.

I concluded that it wasn't so important how big or how little we think our experiences in life are because every circumstance proving His faithfulness is valid, whether we are younger with little life experience or older with lots! Circumstances or experiences are just the illustration of God's goodness and faithfulness in our lives; they're not the center stage. The enemy was very clever to ensure that at a young age I was closed off to the power of testimony.

Revelation 12:11 is a verse I kept hearing a lot at church, which says that we overcome him (our enemy) not only by the blood of the Lamb but also by the power of our testimonies.

In my limited experience, it wasn't just that stories prophesy a good outcome by a faithful God in others' situations. Testimonies give someone the permission and safety they might crave to share their story. It opens a door to bring fear, shame, and guilt into the light where God shines His truth, which reigns over the enemy's lies.

Perhaps it's another ministry we don't think of or recognize at first, but there is real meaning to the adage "a problem shared is a problem halved." I see it now as a gift that is precious and humbling, something not everyone processes.

Los Angeles unlocked a room in me that I couldn't fully get into before. Inside, there were pieces of my personality lying dusty on the floor, but new air was blowing into the room. The dust was coming off, cementing for me on a deeper level that how God designed me wasn't a mistake.

Sitting on the plane, headphones in and music on, happy to have space for my thoughts, the girls came to mind. The mum's longing I held deep in my heart to see my children thrive stirred. Thoughts turned to prayers asking God to help me find ways to show the peace that entered my life, setting a better example of Him to them.

I went back and forth between my music, thoughts, and prayers for some time before the Holy Spirit broke in with the now-familiar pounding in my chest. The thoughts in my head came with a deep sense of understanding in my spirit that they weren't mine. I elbowed my husband to bring him out of his thoughts, explaining how I had some things I felt the Holy Spirit wanted us to do when we got home.

I'm never usually afraid to own my mistakes and say sorry, and that extends as much to our children as to any other relationship. Letting them know when I got it wrong or misunderstood them and asking for their forgiveness was, to me, an important behavior to model. I always believed it stopped us from misunderstanding one another, preventing the enemy from coming between us. The capacity of our daughters to love and forgive me is challenging and inspiring.

When we arrived at the Nashville airport, I texted the girls to see where they were—if they were both at home. As it happened, they were. Once we arrived home and dragged the suitcases upstairs, we popped the kettle on for some tea and gathered our family together, inquiring about their day.

On the car ride from the airport, Adrian and I talked about how to approach them with what the Holy Spirit told me. He felt that since God gave the steps to me, I should take the lead, so I began by filling our daughters in on my experience. They weren't strangers to the moving of the Holy Spirit, especially our eldest daughter, as she'd had opportunities to attend youth camp with our UK church. However, our youngest daughter wasn't old enough then for those, so her experience was more limited.

They listened intently, and as Adrian had his own experiences with God there, they wanted to hear those too. I shared how I reflected on the way home, asking God to help me set a better example of faith for them, when He broke into my thoughts with some steps for us to take. This started with confessing that, as their parents, we had taken our eyes off Jesus over the course of the move, allowing our fears and concerns to appear bigger than Him, and for that, we were sorry.

Tears flowed for all of us. For me, they flowed not because I found it hard to confess or ask for their forgiveness but because of relief. It felt good to bring the weight of guilt I held from not setting the best example I could have into the light, allowing it to be carried away by their hugs of forgiveness.

Sitting back down, I went on to share more of what God was doing in my heart over the years—how it changed my perception of myself and strengthened my faith in Jesus.

I asked if they wanted to talk about the fears and concerns they felt weighed them down. For a moment, they were quiet, and I don't remember who spoke first, but the discussion opened.

As a family, we talked about our fears and anxieties. Adrian and I offered words of encouragement, speaking over them what we saw in them as designed by God. We reassured them that we have hope in a good God, declaring afresh to them that Jesus' name is higher and stronger than anything we ever face.

As our discussion closed, I went to the office to get some paper and pens so we could follow the next part of the Holy Spirit's instructions. This time, we each wrote our struggles on pieces of paper that we didn't share, allowing us to write the things we wanted only God to know—things that were maybe too uncomfortable to share just then.

We placed them in a large trash can, setting light to it. This was a symbol to each other and God that from here on out we believed nothing we faced was bigger than Him. Nothing could hold us captive. We knew we could get through anything with Him and as a family. Watching them burn, we prayed God would help us in our struggles.

Shedding tears of healing felt like God engaged us as a family in a divine moment of restoration. I'm unsure if our daughters understood it fully at the time, and I know they are still walking through that healing every day, but if you ask them, they'll tell you something changed in our home that night.

There was still a lot more to the journey for each of us, apart and together, but the shift was made—not just for them but for generations to come—and I know we all sensed it. It felt like setting new parameters for the enemy, a ring of protection around my family and home.

The final part of God's instructions was to fill our family group chat for thirty days with Scripture, and He had already given me our first one. I don't remember reading this before, so it must have been from the Holy Spirit. I had to look up where it was found, but it was the perfect passage for our new foundation. I could not have picked a better one on my own.

We are pressed on every side by troubles, but we are not crushed. We are perplexed, but not driven to despair. We are hunted down, but never abandoned by God. We get knocked down, but we are not destroyed.

— 2 CORINTHIANS 4:8-9 NLT

It was exactly how we felt: pressed, perplexed, and knocked

out of our comfort zone. Yet the words of hope in these verses brought a perspective shift and comfort to our hearts.

It still makes me tear up to read. The impact of the words still resonates deeply with me, so perfectly fitting our circumstances then. God knew exactly what we needed and when we needed it, and a new atmosphere was established in our home. Chaos was dying in my life, and with it, a beautiful silence arrived where I could hear with new clarity the glorious chatter of heaven for myself and my family, strengthening and cheering us on. The stream of hope began to carry all of us.

CHAPTER 14

WORRY ENDS WHERE
FAITH BEGINS

We loved our new church and community. When I prayed God would break my heart for what broke His, I never imagined the capacity I would have to love so many people. It was a huge departure from how I had made friendships in the past, always discerning how they felt about me before I gave too much of myself away because I didn't want to be blindsided.

I joined the welcome, cleaning, and setup teams. We continued having regular dinner and worship nights, which I was part of the catering team for. This stretched me, cooking for a much larger group than I was used to and helping run the team.

Helping was rewarding and energizing, as it brought new purpose into my life, but I also found so much joy in just being part of the community. It wasn't simply the doing that felt good. Since the community was full of encouragers, it was uplifting to not only receive encouragement but also to be able to give it.

Early on in our new church life, Pastor Dustin, also a songwriter, introduced us to a song he co-wrote: "I Speak Jesus." The lyrics spoke powerfully to the congregation, each of us in the different stages of God making something beautiful with the pieces of our lives and contending for breakthroughs in our families.

We embraced the lyrics with the power of our collective voices, filling the barn we met at with a sound that was full of hope and belief in God's healing. There were so many times I thought the roof might actually lift right off!

The song declares hope, freedom, and healing over fear, anxiety, and depression through the powerful name of Jesus. Sometimes, it felt as if it was written just for my family, as it connected so well to our discussion after our trip to Los Angeles for Gathering.

For the longest time, it was hard to declare Jesus over my family without emotions choking out the words. Tears fell unchecked often, running freely down my face and dripping off my chin.

My husband and I wrapped our arms around each other, combining forces in unison, which made me feel that, even if I couldn't sing it, I was joined with his voice and strength. If our children were near, we pulled them into that embrace—a symbol of our faith and trust in God for them as we declared the words over our family.

That Holy Spirit-charged atmosphere reminded me how worship used to be a strength in our home. I used to play worship music often. Before we moved to the US, I had Matt Redman's "10,000 Reasons" on repeat. I thought back to how the lyrics of the song "Never Once" reassured me while praying about our move.

I missed it, and I needed to bring worship back into our home so God's truths and hope could surround and nurture us continually. It was part of my responsibility to my family to set the atmosphere of our home. I wasn't concerned if it felt like no one paid attention as they went about their tasks; I trusted that the truths of God were powerful enough to shift the atmosphere to hope just by His presence. I believed my family would feel that shift even if subconsciously.

What I did not expect, in the middle of our hope returning, was a conversation with our youngest daughter about how she felt the weight of depression returning. We prayed with her and continually over the next week, asking God to sustain her, and while He did, the week after was tough for her.

She was still seeing her counselor, so professional help was immediately on hand, but I was initially devastated at the news. I had hoped she would never have to face it to this degree again. "Surely," I asked God, "we are in a season of healing and restoration?" I didn't like how it was so hard for her, but then I realized something was different this time: me.

It's not that I felt equipped to handle the situation perfectly, or even close to adequately, but I didn't need to because God could. Back to my mind came the first passage God gave me for our family group chat. It was particularly the last part of 2 Corinthians 4:8—"struck down but not destroyed"—that stuck with me.

Struck down was reality, but *not destroyed* was the truth. This became my prayer: destruction was not coming for her. It gave me hope in the middle of disappointment and worry.

At the end of that week, as I got to church on Sunday, a good friend inquired about our daughter. I hadn't told anyone at this stage, so I knew it could only be God. She went on to tell me that at the beginning of the week she asked God who she should pray for and heard our daughter's name clearly. She was praying faithfully for her every day.

I was awash with gratitude amidst my worries for our daughter, which rose to join 2 Corinthians 4:8's truth, reinforcing my hope. I employed what God had revived in me through worship, using it as a weapon against the enemy to protect her, but having God whisper our daughter's name to someone in our community to pray ahead of time for her brought a new level of strength. God was aware and on the move.

The prayers of faithful friends and the words of hope in that verse united with Adrian's and my prayers. It held up our arms with a new might, yet I was still worried sick. Sitting in prayer one morning, God stirred my heart to question why I worried despite such knowledge of His care and strength.

There's a canvas that hangs at the top of our stairs. It was far from expensive and was bought on a whim. I saw it, thought it had a nice phrase, and knew it would fit our space perfectly. I was pleased when we hung it up, but after that, I paid it very little attention. It would catch my eye from time to time, and I'd think to myself how it was a lovely sentiment. That is, until now.

A few days after God spoke to my heart, I was no further in my investigations of worry. Heading upstairs for some reason, I put my foot on the first step and looked up. The canvas immediately caught my eye, and I saw it with fresh vision. I froze on that step, leaning against the banister for support, as the magnitude of what those words meant settled in my soul: "Worry ends where faith begins."

What a gut punch! I understood in that moment God wanted me to hand my worry over to Him. If I didn't, it would rob the trust I had gained in Him and the new mindset He was giving me. Not doing so would set a bad example for our daughter, especially considering what I'd shared with her and her sister recently. Worry threatened our hope if I continued partnering with it. I prayed simply, "Lord, I'm sorry. Help me let it go."

I dug into why I worried some more to find that I thought if I didn't worry about my children, I was, in some way, being irresponsible. These beautiful daughters of ours were a gift from God, not something I ever took for granted. I knew it was a privilege and joy to have them to love and steward. If I stopped worrying, though, wasn't I giving up some of my parental responsibility?

It's difficult to know how that idea got there. Jesus says in Matthew 6 not to worry, so why did I think worrying was my responsibility? However that thinking got there, it had to go. I couldn't carry the weight of it, and clearly God didn't want me to, or He wouldn't have nudged me toward it in the first place.

The Bible instructs us to cast our burdens on the Lord, and He will sustain us (Psalm 55:2). So, I spent time with Him, asking how to give up worry while not feeling like I was giving up my parental responsibility. Every time I read that canvas, I knew I had to keep pursuing the answer. While simple and bought with very little thought, this canvas was taking me on what I truly believed was a God-intended quest.

It's difficult to watch anyone we love deeply encounter hard times in life. Our first instinct, or at least mine, is to make it better, wishing we could bear it for them. Our hearts hurt and feel like they are being pulled from our chests. A sickness forms deep down in the pit of our stomachs. That's the best way to describe how I felt, worried sick and hurting for my daughter.

I felt strength and hope, yes, and I believed God would sustain her as I continued declaring Scripture and sang worship songs over her, but helplessness and desperation that God would remove her hardship wandered beside them. I had questions too; I'd been here before, feeling helpless, desperate, and worried for my children. Hadn't our daughter been through enough?

In quiet time with the Lord one morning, feeling the weight of those thoughts, I wasn't prepared for what He told me next—another one of those illuminating moments where the truth pierces the soul. Some words from the passage I was reading leapt out at me, and the Holy Spirit followed it with a sense of knowing deep inside it was a message from God. There was a piece of this worry I was digging into that I needed to see.

I'm unsure if I was reading or recapping a sermon I heard, but I was in Genesis 33:12-14, which tells the story of Jacob traveling to see his brother, Esau, for reconciliation. When they finally meet, Esau is keen for them to travel to the next stop together, but Jacob realizes his children and animals are too tired to continue so soon. He tells Esau to go ahead and says that he will follow at a more comfortable pace for his children and livestock.

"At the pace of the children"—the words seemed to jump off the page! In that moment, I felt the Holy Spirit acknowledging that He knew my heart was breaking and I was sick with worry. The very next thought I had, though, was a question: "Is your worry for your children or for you?" Oh boy, I sat dissecting that for a minute!

I wanted to see my children living in the fullness God had for them as early in their lives as possible, not struggling along with the weights of insecurities as I did. There was so much I wanted to save them from. I wanted all the promises of God and happiness for them, and I knew there was absolutely nothing wrong with that.

What I'd missed was that not only was my worry the source of so much fatigue, but I also had to acknowledge a lot of it was for me. It was hard to admit, but deep down I felt it would be so much easier for me if our children could just understand God as I recently started to. The quicker they embraced God fully, the quicker I'd be saved from worry and its weariness.

The more I thought about how difficult it was watching them wander through the difficulties of life, the more I thought about my own. I couldn't deny them their journey; I wouldn't have wanted someone to deny me mine.

There were things I wish I didn't go through, of course, but I wouldn't be here now without those. Even experiencing the rejection of friendship in my teens would have denied me the depth of peace and freedom I felt when God healed my heart and walked me through forgiveness—the knowledge of His character I came into and the depth of love it grew in my life for Him.

I was exhausted from my efforts over the last few years and all the worrying I did. I knew I didn't have the capacity to continue carrying worry like this, but my solution seemed to be that I wanted our children to hurry in their understanding of Jesus instead of trusting God with their lives as much as I now trusted Him with my own.

I knew God wanted to release me of that burden, not just from the revelation itself, but also because, with it, my body released tension. I hadn't realized how much tension I held from my worrying.

I felt myself drawing deeper, slower breaths as a weight inside me began to move. A desire rose up within me to meet God in this, letting Him take that burden. I wrote in my journal, "How do I not worry, Lord? I'd love to know, and I'm trying to choose not to, but it's so hard." Without hesitation, another question dropped into my thoughts: "If I worry, do I think I'm in control?"

That, right there, was the key to freedom. Worrying about circumstances and possible scenarios, coming up with solutions that may or may not be needed, gave me, I thought, some control over my life. I could be prepared for all possibilities, and if none of my worst scenarios came to pass, well, that was a bonus. I believed worrying helped me prepare in life, oblivious to the fact that Psalm 7 says God is the one who gets us ready for life. I thought worrying was the responsible thing to do, but that was another lie weighing me down.

I didn't have the lordship thing down as well as I thought I did; I needed to go deeper. Worry is not from God, yet it managed to present itself as a legitimate problem-solver and a necessary keeper of responsibility. It didn't mean adopting a carefree, nonchalant attitude instead, but I realized worry partnered with control, denying to my family and anyone else that I believed God was faithful, trustworthy, and able to turn things around. It sabotaged my faith and peace, proving I still wasn't trusting Him in all areas of my life.

My children didn't need to know I worried about them; they needed to know I prayed for them and had faith God could be trusted to come through. They needed to know that when I said there was nothing we couldn't get through with God and each other, I really meant it. I knew I couldn't slip back into my old patterns!

I did not want to lose the progress I'd made and go backwards. I needed to pull together all He had taught me, leaning into Him even more. Worry had to end so my faith could rise, setting the best example for my children that I could.

I became more intentional in remembering my past victories and using them to fuel my faith for this battle—focusing on the fact that if He came through before, then He would again. Our family was called on this journey to America together, and I had to believe beyond myself, safe in the knowledge that He'd also faithfully carry our children to victory. One of us wasn't more important or purposed than the other, nor was age a factor. God was trustworthy to each of us just as He'd shown me years before. I had to trust He'd take care of our "Elis."

Worry had never won anything for us, and when my agenda accompanied it, I enthusiastically took every little opportunity to bring a "sermon" to my daughter. I must admit, I still understood very little about depression at the time, so it was a process of learning to back off that temptation, instead inviting the Holy Spirit to prompt me when to speak and when not to (both are equally important).

Sometimes the silence in just being together spoke the loudest. Other times, giving space spoke louder. It took me a while to realize that all my "sermons" were too overwhelming for my young listener.

A while before, I read the book *Words from the Hill*, written by our friend Stu. In it, he highlighted how we should practice listening to hear, not listening to respond. That's exactly what I was doing: listening to respond in light of my agenda. I needed to develop the art of listening to hear—to discern when and if to respond at all.

My daughter and I have had honest conversations about that period of her life, at *her* pace. God had a very specific way in which He wanted to journey with her, even if I found it hard to accept. My responsibility was supporting her however she needed—offering reassurance that she would get through this and praying for her. I needed to trust God with the lives of our children just as I had come to trust Him with my life.

When I learned to step out of the way, swapping worry and control for trusting Him with my daughters—when I went to war in the spiritual realm through prayer and worship, no longer trying to control the narrative—He could move. All the time I partnered with worry, I was blinkered. As the year came to an end, things had begun improving for our daughter again. Not perfect, but God was in control, and she was finding her inner strength and moving forward.

Not having had the capacity before to think about college, my husband and I thought now was a good time to reopen that conversation. She wasn't wholly open to it at first but eventually decided to go with us to look at a few local ones with film programs.

The first one we visited was potentially the most expensive! During the tour, we were separated from our group because we talked too long with one of the tutors. On finding this out, he asked if we'd like a private tour. As we looked behind the scenes, I watched our daughter's eyes light up.

On our own later that day, Adrian and I talked about that light we saw—how it warmed our hearts—and we both had a growing sense that this was where she was meant to go. We discussed our financial situation and how we knew it would be more than a stretch to cover the potential fees. It would take a miracle, and if we were right, we would have to trust God would provide.

Our daughter visited a few other colleges, but she didn't talk as enthusiastically about them as she did the first. When the offer letters arrived and she had to decide, it was clear that although she really wanted to go to the first one, she considered accepting the less expensive option. We kept telling her that God would provide and that she should go with the program she felt most excited about. We kept trusting and praying.

I'm not sure how long it was until one afternoon she came home from school to tell me how her film and broadcasting teacher, knowing about her college applications, shared that the smallest college she visited was being bought out by her first choice.

We called the administration office to check, and sure enough, a very helpful lady confirmed it, advising us to accept the offer from the smaller college, as those fees would be honored by her first choice. The miraculous timing of that purchase was undeniable—God provided! Our trust in Him was honored, and our prayers were answered in a way far better than any of my "sermons." We were all in wonder at Him; worry wouldn't have added anything to that.

I look at the canvas at the top of our staircase differently now. Its simple words fill me with gratitude every time I read them, a reminder of God's goodness and what it is to have faith over worry or my agenda. He chose a seemingly insignificant yet profound little canvas bought on a whim to use mightily in building a stream of faith for the good of my family.

CHAPTER 15

POWERFUL PRAYERS

It was a few weeks into the year 2020, and we were consumed with all things wedding. I was knee-deep in English ivy, forget-me-nots, and baby's breath as my floor filled up with completed table centerpieces. I burned my fingers with hot glue more times than I could remember and spent a lot of my week at Hobby Lobby, but I was loving it.

Then news started reporting a virus spreading around the world. Countries were closing because of it.

When it finally affected the UK, we were devastated that our family and friends there would not be able to attend, but we still held onto the hope that our daughter's wedding would be able to go ahead with local friends.

But things got worse. We began hearing that, in some states, hospitals struggled to look after the sick. Stay-at-home orders were issued for residents to stop the spread of the disease. I got a feeling that Tennessee would not make it to April without having to introduce the same order.

It was the topic of conversation every day, and our eldest daughter's anxiety and disappointment grew. As we passed mid-

March, I thought of how I would feel if it were my wedding day. I would probably want to bring my wedding forward even if only a handful of people could attend so I wouldn't be confined to my parent's home past our wedding date if stay-at-home orders were issued. I talked it over with Adrian, and he felt the same. We contacted our pastor to see how he felt, and he also agreed.

Then came the difficult task of talking with our daughter and soon-to-be son-in-law. I knew they'd be disappointed on a level I couldn't understand, and I felt completely gutted that our daughter wasn't going to have the day she hoped or planned for. She was devastated and decided to sleep on it, but the next day, with resignation in her voice, she told me that she and her fiancé agreed it was probably the best option.

We postponed the venue, caterer, and everything else connected to the original wedding date for a year. Some amazing, talented friends in our community rallied to decorate our church's little barn, making bouquets from the flowers that had not yet made it to the centerpieces, and a dear friend took pictures.

It was so far from what I imagined our daughter's wedding day would be and from what she'd dreamed of, but it was nonetheless beautiful. It was, in fact, the very last event we held in the barn for some time, as stay-at-home orders came to Tennessee within days, and the church switched services to Zoom.

My dad quoted Ecclesiastes 9:11 to us while growing up, reminding us how sometimes, as the world happens around us, we are caught up in things we didn't choose and can't control, but God is always near. I thought about this as we drove home from the little wedding service, grieving what wasn't to be and the lost opportunity to spend precious time with our overseas family.

Tears flowed with disappointment and bewilderment at why things had to be as they were, but Dad's words reminded me to keep trusting in what I knew: God was in control and ever-present.

I didn't have the detailed view or big picture for the world God had—our world is broken, and people make immoral or imperfect decisions every day—but I trusted that even though we were caught up in this period of time, God would give her the day she dreamed of. I had no doubt that He cared as much about our daughter's wedding as she, her fiancé, and her family did.

I believe the feeling I sensed about Tennessee soon following the other states in shutting down was God's nudge to action. He knew what was around the corner. I'm glad I knew Him well enough to act on it, realizing how much my faith and trust in God had grown—allowing me to rest in Him quickly rather than give in to worry or wallow in disappointment.

Our church had only met together officially for five months when we shifted to online services, so when it was announced that we'd have Thursday prayer nights on Zoom, I was shocked to find myself wanting to attend.

As much as worship always passionately tugged at my heart, prayer did not. It's not that I didn't pray—I did more so over the last several years—but I had always struggled with consistency, so a lot of guilt circled my prayer life. I was much more consistent in prayer when a personal crisis hit or a big decision needed to be made, but when life was comfortable, my prayer life slipped.

To be honest, in these unusual circumstances, with everything around us closed, Zoom prayer nights were something to fill our time with, but more importantly, for me, it was an opportunity to feel connected to those I had grown to love in such a short time.

As much as I felt guilty about my private prayer life, I feared public prayer. No one else heard private prayers; they were between God and me. But public prayers could be judged by others, and I was fixated on that. Yet here I was, in this new church community, learning to walk in new streams, providing God with the perfect opportunity for another challenge!

I understood by now that for God to heal me or bring freedoms to my life, it often necessitated being taken out of my comfort zone. I didn't always like it, but I knew better things were on the other side of the process.

The challenges since our move to the US meant, out of necessity, my personal prayer life was more consistent, but nothing about praying publicly had changed. I had a misconceived idea there was a "proper" way to do it.

I'd often heard prayers criticized, which left a lasting impression. I feared getting it wrong so much, allowing the fear of what others might think to attach to it over the years. I became such an expert at evading it, melting into the background, that no one had asked me to publicly pray in years.

A prayer meeting was something I had spent years avidly avoiding, yet there I was, willingly joining a Zoom prayer meeting under the mistaken notion I could continue to stay in the background. Nothing could have prepared me for the format those evenings took.

At the first one, we began with a short time of worship before a few people, who were asked beforehand, would unmute their screens to pray over their assigned subject. Even though that format can sound clinical, it was strengthening to be united in an unsteady time. I began to really look forward to these evenings. The Holy Spirit moved among us on those Thursday nights, and powerful prayers were prayed for our nation, church, and one another.

I didn't seem to notice—how I missed the implication of it, I don't know—that people were being asked in turn, a few each week, to participate. I still thought I was safely in the background. But God knew me well, and after years without church community, I enthusiastically jumped right in. I didn't stop to calculate any "cost" to me. I don't think I cared… Until it was our turn to pray!

The day before the next prayer meeting, I was up in the morning, getting ready for the day as usual. My husband was already up and working from home. He took a call from one of the church leaders, immediately coming upstairs to share the contents of the discussion. We'd been together thirty-five years at this point, so I knew by the somber look on his face he was about to tell me something I wouldn't like. Sure enough, we were asked to pray.

Also knowing me well, he didn't give an answer, saying that he would ask me what I wanted to do first. I laughed awkwardly to cover the sinking feeling inside as fear reached for me once again.

On the one hand, I wanted to give God my yes, and on the other, I was panic-stricken. I felt the rug was yanked suddenly from beneath me, my brain teetering about in a daze. This wasn't how it was supposed to go. What happened to being in the background?

Fear battled hard in my thoughts. I loved the background, didn't I? I spent a lot of my life hiding there. Being in the background was safety—expectations were low, so you couldn't mess up or be noticed enough to have to try.

I had no perception of just how much fear had infiltrated my prayer life. Just like in other areas of my life, I didn't want to be judged if I made a mistake. I feared fumbling my words or my mind going blank. What if my theology wasn't correct, my words were too pleading, or they weren't full of enough faith? Pride was entangled in it. What if I let people down when they asked me to pray and let myself down?

To make matters worse, people asked to pray now on our

Zoom calls were no longer given a topic to pray about but rather were asked to pray about what they felt the Holy Spirit laid on their hearts. It was manna for my soul to watch the Holy Spirit "sync up" those nights, weaving a theme through each person's prayer from their respective homes. It was amazing and powerful, but now it presented double the fear and anxiety because it wasn't just praying out loud that gripped me with panic.

I didn't want to be the one to go off the Holy Spirit's script. I didn't want to risk being the one out of sync, the fly in the ointment, and it played like a loop in my head. Fear was stepping into the driver's seat, as it so often had before, making me question if I would hear the Holy Spirit like I did in Los Angeles. My walls of self-protection were ready to go up. I could feel it, and fighting felt overwhelming.

I asked my husband to give me time to think about it, but I felt sick to my stomach. So much so that I broke out in a cold sweat. My mind turned against me, instantly flooding with anxiety. I didn't think I had the strength to push through the physical symptoms. It was too hard. Did I even want to?

Eventually, wanting to rid myself of those physical manifestations of panic and wanting my body to feel at peace, I gave in and said no. I completely caved and left it to my husband to carry us that evening, and I tried moving on with my day.

God, of course, had other plans because, from this point, my morning was needled with the recurring thought that even though I'd made such progress in my spiritual life, I must have been a constant disappointment to God. I tried hard not to ask Him just in case I didn't like the answer!

As my morning continued, I got ready to begin praying, as promised, for a friend while she was to be in an appointment. Sitting there, praying for her, the Holy Spirit unexpectedly broke into my thoughts to say He wanted me to pray at the prayer meeting. I quickly dismissed it, though! I'd already said no, and my husband was on that task for us. Right now, I just needed to concentrate on praying for my friend.

The Holy Spirit broke into my prayers, and again, I tried pushing His words aside. On His third attempt, I heard Him so clearly in my head: "I want you to pray, and I want you to pray my name, Jesus." I knew it was God because I would never tell myself that, plus it came with the now very familiar Holy Spirit-pounding feeling in my chest, but I still hesitated to say yes.

Wrestling, I thought it was a good idea to remind God how I was there to pray for my friend, asking if maybe I could think about it later. Added to that, it occurred to me that I couldn't just bring one word to a prayer meeting. People would be expecting lots of words!

But as soon as my mind strung that thought together, the familiar pounding in my chest became stronger. I heard Him reply, "My name may be just one word, but it is not one thing. It is everything."

Everything suspended! I sat humbled as the power of those words and the revelation they brought permeated my entire being. Nothing else matters; anything else pales in significance because Jesus is everything. I was singing His name in what had become our church anthem, "I speak Jesus," yet here I was, putting the fear of others that I had been living free from in other areas of my life against God's request.

I was utterly compelled in that moment to change my answer, and when I'd finished praying for my friend, I went downstairs to fill my husband in on my Holy Spirit encounter and my change of decision. Somewhat surprised, of course, but proud of me for changing my mind, he reassured me it would be okay and let our prayer group leader know.

As I began to speak that night, I asked the Holy Spirit to help me not mess up, and I drew strength from my husband's faith in me and his presence beside me. Despite raging anxiety,

I started by explaining how the Holy Spirit encountered me earlier in the day because I still felt I needed to say more than one word.

When I came to say His name, I felt prompted to speak it out over fear and anxiety in our community. The moment I did, it came out loudly in the room. Everyone on the call seemed to disappear.

It was just me and the Holy Spirit, and the words that came next were a declaration and reminder of who Jesus is to anyone hurting or lost or confused: savior, protector, healer, guide, and king.

In His name, there is forgiveness, belonging, courage, encouragement, refuge, endurance, victory, strength, and wisdom for everything we face, and it's full of love, peace, joy, and hope. It felt like I was declaring with power and clarity all the things my soul knew about Him, everything He had shown Himself to be for me.

I was surprised by the loudness. There was a power behind the words, not my power but God's. I couldn't hold them back. Just like I was propelled out of my seat to be prayed for by my pastors during the season of infertility, these words propelled themselves from my mouth.

Immediately afterward, I felt relief to get through it, but in the days that followed, I was in awe yet again of God for the way He gave me words in the moment (when that was something I feared) and for His never-ending patience despite my resistance. He wasn't out to force me just for the sake of it. He knew that by persevering with me, I would receive something new in my life and a deeper understanding of Him.

Every time I retell this story, I feel the power of that revelation all over again, and it moves me. I thought I understood there was power and authority in the name of Jesus. I saw it at work and experienced it in my life, but it hit differently that day. Fear was like an onion, with so many layers, but as I surrendered and trusted Him, He removed each of them, one by one.

In my early years of study, I learned that when children are small, they learn the basic concepts of things, like science, through play. As they get older and their understanding widens and develops, they revisit those concepts again and again in more complex ways until they understand them at deeper levels. I thought about how true that was of my spiritual life too.

A hammer of knowledge came down within me that day, and many lingering lies and doubts the enemy could still taunt me with flew up in splinters, losing their footing. Something new from God replaced the space they occupied.

I took hold of the authority I had in Jesus' name in a new way. The weeds of fear had been able to spread in the soil of my heart, so even though knowledge of my authority in Jesus was seeded, it couldn't properly take root. But now a new understanding of my authority through Jesus could finally grow, lasting a lifetime. The greatest power to overcome this world lived in me, and demons trembled at the mention of His name.

The revived me knew that to have a greater depth of peace, the kind that surpasses understanding, I had to fully grasp all the power that was mine in His name. I can't say every time I was asked to pray after that was a breeze. Like things so often can be, even after a revelation like this, it was a battle to get my body and mind to catch up to the knowledge in my spirit. I was entering another process.

For months during that process, I spent time with God, writing my prayers before I prayed them in public. Hearing from God in my writing felt safe and familiar, but sometimes anxiety still made itself known, and I made multiple trips to the bathroom before the meeting started!

At first, I was concerned people would think I was weak or disingenuous, but God never made me feel that way. I sensed if writing out my prayers was what I needed at the time, He would be okay with that. It didn't make my prayers any less acceptable to Him, and I knew that mattered more than anyone's opinion.

Fumbling my words or paraphrasing Scripture didn't bother Him either. He saw the intention of my heart, my determination to choose Him over fear, and graciously gave me amazing friends who loved and supported me at every twist and turn. They never seemed to tire of listening to me talk about how hard it was at times to push through my thoughts and fears; they never made me feel like I should just get over it. They encouraged and strengthened me, alongside our community on those Zoom prayer nights, with patience and kindness as I battled my way to victory.

Something else needled me, though: my voice could get loud. Being loud was one of the things I came to dislike about myself over the years. I knew I could be the loudest voice at the table or laugh in the room, and not everyone was comfortable with that.

At family get-togethers growing up, everyone talked at once. If you wanted to have your say on a subject, you had to be louder than everyone else to be heard. I always loved the energy and buoyancy of that chatter. Some people need to learn how to project their voice, but I never had that issue; it always came naturally.

Of course, the older I got, the more I understood the need to be sensitive to my surroundings. Not every situation was one to be loud and demonstrative in, but I disliked it, and it was one of the things I'd wondered if my husband's bandmates also disliked.

I tried to control it through the years, but as soon as I started relaxing in the company or surroundings I was in, it came bounding back. The level of annoyance and frustration I felt at my loss of restraint was often powerful enough to make me feel sick to my stomach for days, consuming me with the concern I probably would not be invited back.

I hated the battle of it, ruining perfectly lovely evenings out and constantly asking whoever was with me, usually my husband, "How'd I do? Was I too loud or too much?" It never occurred to me to ask God if He had any purpose for it since He gave me my voice! I wished so hard it was quieter or that I could control it better. Every encounter added to my self-disdain.

It was another hold of the enemy's that God wanted to expose in this process—one that had fed into feelings of being "too much" for most of my life. In surrender to Him through prayer, He showed me He had purpose even for this!

The enemy's foothold here cost me in my self-worth—another thing keeping me quiet and in hiding. As I wrestled with the volume that my voice reached when the Holy Spirit moved me, people within our community continuously encouraged me. It was surprising that no one mentioned it was too loud, yet I felt compelled to apologize for it.

What also surprised me was how most people didn't remember the words I spoke either; they remembered the presence of the Holy Spirit instead. I may have been the one speaking the prayer, but our spirits were mightily joined together as we stood in agreement, contending for our friends, church, and nation. Ironically, though different from how I thought it would be, I *was* hidden in the background as God came to the fore!

I don't brag about that in any way; it simply made me want to let God take the reins more in my life. He had purpose for my voice, and the enemy wasn't keeping me from it any longer.

I didn't just say yes to praying publicly; it was also to continuing the journey of healing with God. "Yes" was my only part—the rest was all Him. He was so faithful in responding to my obedience and tender with my surrender, returning to me a blessing of freedom and understanding I couldn't have imagined. God continued to reclaim my life, showing me the purposes He had for how He made me. Though it was still painful at times to uncover them, the warmth of His light gave me refuge and resolve to recover.

My personal prayer life changed too. I felt more motivated to carve out time to pray at home. My prayers were bolder as I reclaimed my authority in Jesus, and more often they looked like the prayers I prayed in my daughter's room in Colorado when depression first showed up.

Almost a year later, as those Zoom prayer nights came to an end, I kept hearing in my mind, "The training wheels are coming off." On the last of those nights, our pastor spoke similar words over me, confirming, as I suspected, it was indeed a season of training.

God not only led me back to more powerful prayers, but He also broke barriers in the process. He deepened the experience of prayer, freeing me from places where fear and a lack of self-worth still held me hostage.

God took something I disliked deeply about myself—something I spent a lifetime trying to control—and brought me to a place of understanding its purpose. He showed me what He could do with it when I placed it in His hands for His glory.

The lie I held for so long—that prayer was difficult, overwhelming, and up for judgment—was broken. It didn't matter how my prayers looked or sounded, written down or spoken in the moment, or whether they were deep longings or simple pleas for help. Prayers are powerful, and not one of them is missed by God. I grew in confidence that heaven was listening, and so was I, as the voice of the Holy Spirit became its own stream in my life.

However hard I felt this journey was—however much shorter I wished it could have been—answers to prayer came at their appointed time. A new and firm belief that there was no limit to what God could do with surrender and the creative ways He could heal developed.

I don't write my prayers out anymore when praying

publicly, and I don't always have to be asked to pray. When I'm nudged by the Holy Spirit, I can pray as needed. Sometimes, though, that fear of failing still threatens to creep back in and stop me.

God, though, has never let me down any time I have said yes in the face of it. He provides strength in my weaknesses to bring about His greater purposes, even when I do it with fear at my heels, and in it, He gets to shine.

CHAPTER 16

JESUS FOR MY FAMILY

It had been quite the journey for us—one I never expected or thought I needed. I left the UK thinking I understood what Isaiah 43:18-19 meant for our family.

> Forget the former things; do not dwell on the past. See, I am doing a new thing! Now it springs up; do you not perceive it? I am making a way in the wilderness and streams in the wasteland.

I interpreted that "new thing" as what my husband was bringing to his new role, new opportunities to bring worship music to the world, and resourcing the church. As for our daughters and me, I thought it referred to the new culture we would encounter, new opportunities we'd have, and, ultimately, the new life we would build in the midst of those.

It had never occurred to me that God also intended this season to revive my spiritual life, which had become a wilderness over the years. He was often drowned out by the noise of my life at the beginning, and I missed much of His love and protection when things didn't look how I pictured, yet He continued in His long-suffering, patient nature to uphold me—capturing my attention.

As for "streams in the wasteland," I assumed those words meant God went ahead of us to make the practicalities of settling in easier. It wasn't on my radar that this wilderness season would also be a spiritual journey of healing I so desperately needed, but God knew.

He proved how much He cared, bringing life-giving streams to the wilderness of my heart, overflowing with such love, kindness, and goodness, ultimately leading me back to Him. These waters lapped at my family's feet too, bringing hope and restoration.

I used to bring God into situations only so far before I took over, doing things in my own strength and ability, controlling circumstances and outcomes out of self-protection because I didn't know Him well enough to trust He would take care of me.

I used to think all my doubts—toing and froing in my faith—would eventually disappoint God to the point He'd give up on me. But over the years, He has shown me I can never be a disappointment to Him; He loves unconditionally, even knowing where I'd fail or mess up.

When hope was all but gone in our home and despair was taking its place, God, with great tenderness and kindness, nudged me to the revelation that to make a change, I first had to be willing to change. I've always believed that the tone of any organization is set by its leader, and family is no different.

In a slowed-down season, God had great intent, and I have found Jesus' words in Matthew 6:31-34 (MSG) encapsulate that better than mine ever could.

What I'm trying to do here is get you to relax, to not be so preoccupied with *getting*, so you can respond to God's *giving*. People who don't know God and the way he works fuss over these things, but you both know God and how He works. Steep your life in God-reality, God-initiative, God-provisions. Don't worry about missing out. You'll find all your everyday human concerns will be met. Give your entire attention to what God is doing right now, and don't get worked up about what may or may not happen tomorrow. God will help you deal with whatever hard things come up when the time comes.

Even if I didn't always understand what we walked through, He proved Himself (though He didn't have to) to be good and faithful in everything. We were never abandoned.

A few years ago, my family watched the fruits from that season when I suddenly found myself shouldering a time of illness. In one week, I went from serving with our church as we hosted Gathering to being barely able to walk, stand, or sit without excruciating pain.

No matter what was prescribed, nothing eased the pain, and eventually it was decided I should have a hysterectomy. I was anxious, of course, but the night before surgery, I had a dream where I was at Jesus' feet, my head on His lap, and a great sense of peace settled on me. As the different doctors and nurses hooked me up to various drips or administered medicine, I kept that image with me, and it calmed my anxiousness.

Initially interpreting that image to mean the surgery would fix the pain, I was shocked and disappointed as I dragged my pain-filled body to my follow-up appointment—the effort of which was nauseating, registering low blood pressure. I knew something wasn't right. There was no way I could drive or handle light housework as I should have been able to at this stage of recovery.

Eventually, I was referred to another specialist who discovered where the issue stemmed from. I received the diagnosis of a chronic illness with no cure, and we began a trial and error of diet changes and medication regimens. It was four months before I was able to leave the house, shuffle into church, and sit semi-comfortably through a service. It was a year before I could go to a store even for something simple like milk or bread.

Despite the dream not panning out as I had hoped, I didn't feel the need to throw a tantrum over it not going my way. This was going to go God's way, and I was determined to utilize everything He had taught me from our previous season as best I could. Whether it seems foolish or not, I felt I shouldn't research the diagnosis either. In my spirit, I sensed doing so would take my eyes from Him, and I'd descend into panic.

Instead, I set my heart on prayer, worship, and study, building my faith to keep me from worry and despair. As much as I was able, watching our church service at home, I'd drag myself to my feet for a few bars of a worship song, telling God that if standing to worship Him was all I could ever manage again, I would be content. He would still be good and ever worthy of my praise, and I can honestly say I meant it; I truly believed it at my core.

I had my moments, of course, of overwhelm, unsure of what my future looked like, but I took it one day at a time, fixing my eyes on Him. I wasn't second-guessing God's plan, which helped me see my dream differently too, leaning on it to carry me through the season and not just the one procedure, as I had first thought. It was a testing season, and I found that more often than not, I was at peace in it—glad for the opportunity it gave me to prove myself to Him just as He had proved Himself to me.

I added crocheting to my days so I felt productive—a small, practical thing that brought me joy in the waiting amidst a lot of movies—but ultimately, the season became about Him and not my circumstances, as I'd so easily fallen foul of before.

I couldn't help but reflect on our journey as a family since we had moved to the US. Our eldest daughter arrived with a promise God would restore all she had lost but was grieving it hard. She lost the familiarity that anchored her, enduring so much loneliness the first three years, often worried she'd never find her footing in America and her future would be bleak. Yet, in a very visible job in a coffee shop, she gained friends and met her husband.

Despite the changes to their wedding day, we celebrated with a ceremony of blessing at the original venue one year later, followed by a wonderful reception as close to the one originally planned as possible, as our UK family and friends still couldn't travel. It was a beautiful and joyful day. God was faithful in His promise to her.

We have been privileged to worship with them in our church community every week, and we were overjoyed to welcome our grandson not long ago.

Celebrating at our favorite restaurant, it was not lost on me that I sat in this same restaurant twenty-eight years before while on a work trip with Adrian, pouring out bitter disappointments at the mounting years of infertility. Yet here we were, engulfed by the faithfulness of God, welcoming the next generation! God was faithful in His promises to us.

Our youngest daughter arrived differently in America; she was excited and looking forward to the opportunities it offered. She loved movies, adventures, and dreaming. It should have been a perfect fit for her, but instead, over time, the light of that excitement went out.

She was expected to take her new life by the horns and thrive, not live with the weight of shattered dreams and disappointment, wondering if life would be worth the effort at all. But God provided an opportunity for college like we couldn't have imagined, where she was able to enroll and excel in a great film program, bringing good and stable friendships into her life.

She lives with some of those friends now, and her light continues to grow as independence stretches her. She shows such grace and strength as she meets the challenges of it with courage. In her community of friends, she is daring to dream again. God was faithful to her confident expectation of hope.

Although life is still not perfect, as a family, we have come a long way. Each of our daughters is building on what God's faithfulness brought about in their lives, and it's a privilege to watch. He is shaping their futures in very different ways, and Adrian and I are so proud of them.

I never thought I'd say I'm glad for that season—as I honestly wouldn't want to repeat it—but I am. I'm grateful it eventually sent me running to God for the restoration I now have in my life and the hope and strength my faith continues to give me and my family. I don't relish the pain of God's pruning and pressing, but I've learned that on the other side there's a profound breath to be drawn, where rest and peace can be taken in at incredible depths. I welcome the beauty of the other side.

During my period of illness, journaling continued to be one of my most treasured gifts. It began like a tributary, which over time became a stream of great significance, reconnecting my heart to God. I had learned to hear His voice again there, even if I was too focused on circumstances to see it at the time. He had cared for me there, signposting His faithfulness, and the pages held so much gratitude.

The level of thankfulness birthed in that weighty season had also formed its own stream, and I leaned on it during that intense period of illness. We used to sing in church from Psalm 100:4, "I will enter His gates with thanksgiving in my heart. I will enter his courts with praise." The Passion Translation puts the latter half as "come right into His presence with thanksgiving." I wanted to continually access His presence, to walk with peace in that testing season.

With time to study, I came across an article that said with gratitude, more contentment and joy enter our lives. It helps us feel fewer negative emotions, we handle difficulties better, and it may even help us form deeper relationships. I loved the idea of psychology using biblical principles, even if they didn't recognize it—further proof to me that God knew exactly what we needed to succeed when He designed us. I didn't want to underestimate the power of thankfulness so hard-won on my journey; I wanted to put it to good use.

Eventually my doctors found a regimen that started working, and as the pain eased, mobility returned. It was an uphill battle. The pain was often triggered by things that couldn't be identified. Then, my doctor's office called to say they were closing. I was disappointed but not initially concerned, resigned to continue with another office they suggested, but my first two experiences there were disheartening.

Disappointment and worry knocked hard at my door, but I was resolved to keep trusting God, using all the tools at my disposal to keep them out. As I continued praying for healing and direction, I researched new options and settled on a place with great testimonials, though I had to wait several months to be seen.

While I waited, I leaned on the power of my prayer language, finding it gave me incredible strength, especially on harder days. Over time, I sensed the Holy Spirit tell me that my healing would come in stages.

I talked to God honestly about how I felt and what I longed for, revealing the kind of relationship I wanted to continue having with Him. Even though He already knew my needs and desires, I was confident now that like any parent, He wanted to be invited into them—just like Adrian and I still want our children to know they can come to us with their struggles because we are stronger together in prayer, counsel, and faith than apart. I wanted God to know I valued our relationship and had complete trust and faith in Him with this new challenge I had entered.

A few weeks before the appointment, during worship at church, someone unexpectedly came to pray with me. As she prayed for healing from "head to toe," what felt like an electric charge went through my body from… head to toe. I wish I could say I sensed wrongly about my healing and was instantly healed, but that wasn't the case. Instead, God met me powerfully in a familiar way He had in the past, letting me know I was seen. This time, I had no doubts that He'd carry me through whatever those stages of healing looked like.

At the new doctor's office, in that very desirable gown, I sat, anxious for a good outcome. Waiting, I prayed, and a beautiful sense of peace came into the room, like I'd experienced in my dream before the hysterectomy surgery, confirming I was in the right place.

The appointment couldn't have gone better, and I left with new medications, more supplement-based than chemical, and over the months that followed, I slowly reintegrated into life beyond the four walls of my home.

Today, I'm not running any marathons, but life looks so different than it did when the illness began in September 2021. At the beginning, I wasn't sure what to expect going forward, but by May 2023, I was on a trip back to the UK with our family and a few friends. It was a challenging season, unlike any other in the past. Peace stayed close, hope never left, and God remained the same: faithful.

I'm grateful to be able to look back over quite a few seasons in my life. Some were longer than others, containing hardships and pain I'd rather not have encountered; some were overflowing with joy; and some had both. But each one has been a spiritual adventure with God in one way or another.

A few years ago, as our creative team met at church, the Holy Spirit gave me a word for them during worship. Since then, it has not been far from my mind. *Your release is in your response!*

As I have thought about it and how it relates personally, I believe it encapsulates what God wanted me to understand for the past seasons of my life and those still to come: He always has what I need, but I hold the key to surrender.

Surrender isn't just where my greatest rest and peace reside but also where my greatest access to Him flows. Luke 11:18 says we are blessed when we hear and obey, and though I struggled to step into its stream at first, He used my small, stumbling steps of surrender to take me back to the greatest stream of all: Jesus.

The water He brought to my life when I felt useless, lonely, and hopeless sat first on the parched, dry ground of my heart before it could seep into the crevices of my life and spill over, but God never gave up. As streams began forming in my wilderness, they flowed directly to Him.

I no longer need to avoid the question, "Who am I?" anymore. I know far beyond the doubts I once had that I am His, He is mine, and His continuing banner over me is love. It is by far the greatest honor and privilege to share my story and to bring Jesus the glory—something my doubts would never have let me confidently do before.

Perhaps you find yourself in a season that doesn't make sense, full of unexpected challenges and disappointments, worried you're discounted or if God is still with you and sees you.

May my story be a testament to what He can do in the wilderness seasons we all inevitably walk through when we take a step toward Him. I encourage you to take that step, allowing Him to bring you the streams you need on your journey. No matter how lost, hopeless, or undeserving you feel, His faithful streams are always accessible and able to lead you back to Him.

Keep trusting in the Lord and do what is right in his eyes.
Fix your heart on the promises of God and you will dwell
in the land, feasting on his faithfulness. Find your delight
and true pleasure in YAHWEH, and he will give you what
you desire the most. Give God the right to direct your

life, and as you trust him along the way, you'll find he pulled it off perfectly!

— PSALM 37:3-5 TPT

So let's *do* it—full of belief, confident that we're presentable inside and out. Let's keep a firm grip on the promises that keep us going. He always keeps his word.

— HEBREWS 10:22-23 MSG

FURTHER ENCOURAGEMENT FOR YOUR JOURNEY

30 DAYS OF SCRIPTURE

This book came from the thirty days of Scripture that God asked me to post in our family group chat. After several months, I realized our daughters were unlikely to go searching back through our messages to look for them when they needed encouragement.

As Christmas that year approached, I desired to put those verses into a book as a gift for them. I was disappointed in myself when January rolled around that I didn't have time to do that. Feeling regret, I had a thought, which I attribute to the Holy Spirit, that I should collect them in a book alongside my testimony for my family (and in case they would be helpful to others), so here we are!

My testimony represents the oil I want to pour onto the altar of this book, which, for me, marks a season of my life where He reaffirmed His love for me and I for Him—breaking unshakeable new ground in my life.

Thank you for being here. I hope you have found encouragement from my story for your walk of faith. Whatever stream you feel you need to step into, even if it's just to journal for the first time, I hope you have been inspired to trust Him for the expedition ahead. I know He will prove Himself to be the joy of your surrender.

I pray these Scriptures not only encourage you on your journey but also keep you connected to the greatest life-giving stream of all: Jesus.

1. This is the beginning! No matter what pressures we've faced at this point, God is present, still holding and strengthening us. We are not abandoned. As the Holy Spirit dropped this verse into my heart, I knew it was the truth I should start with.

> We are hard pressed on every side, but not crushed; perplexed, but not in despair; persecuted, but not abandoned; struck down, but not destroyed.
>
> — 2 CORINTHIANS 4:8-9

2. He values you! Every detail of your life, every worry or concern, and whatever difficulty you face matters to Him enormously. You are not alone.

> What is the value of your soul to God? Could your worth be defined by any amount of money? God doesn't abandon or forget even the small sparrow he has made. How then could he forget or abandon you? What about the seemingly minor issues of your life? Do they matter to God? Of course they do! So, you never need to worry, for you are more valuable to God than anything else in this world.
>
> — LUKE 12:6-7 TPT

3. His love never changes! God reassures us that nothing we

face changes how He feels toward us. He promises nothing has the power to separate us from that love.

> There is no power above us or beneath us—no power that could ever be found in the universe that can distance us from God's passionate love, which is lavished upon us through our Lord Jesus, the Anointed One!
>
> — ROMANS 8:39 TPT

4. Comfort for anxiety! When anxiousness surrounds you, He's right there. The comfort of His presence carries all that you need, and with it comes joy as you rest in Him.

> When I said, "My foot is slipping," your unfailing love, LORD, supported me. When anxiety was great within me, your consolation brought me joy.
>
> — PSALM 94:18-19

5. Worship changes our perspective! Everything changes in His presence. There is so much peace in His majesty, and all we need to enter is our thanksgiving and praise. Be encouraged to worship Him no matter your circumstances. He is faithful in keeping His promises.

> Lift up a great shout of joy to YAHWEH! Go ahead and do it—everyone, everywhere! Worship YAHWEH with gladness. Sing your way into his presence with joy! And realize what this really means—we have the privilege of worshipping YAHWEH our God. For he is our Creator and we belong to him. We are the people of his pleasure. You can pass through his open gates with the password of praise. Come right into his presence with thanksgiv-

ing. Come bring your thank offering to him and affectionately bless his beautiful name! For YAHWEH is always good and ready to receive you. He's so loving that it will amaze you—so kind it will astound you! And he is famous for his faithfulness toward all. Everyone knows our God can be trusted, for he keeps his promises to every generation!

— PSALM 100 TPT

6. Circumstances won't overpower you! He promises that even our worst circumstances will never overcome us because we belong to Him. He is our Savior.

Don't be afraid, I've redeemed you. I've called your name. You're mine. When you're in over your head, I'll be there with you. When you're in rough waters, you will not go down. When you're between a rock and a hard place, it won't be a dead end—because I am GOD, your personal God, the Holy of Israel, your Savior. I paid a huge price for you... *That's* how much you mean to me! *That's* how much I love you!

— ISAIAH 43:2-4 MSG

7. The antidote to stress and worry! When we replace our stress and worry with prayer—taking the details of our concerns to Him in faith and thankfulness—we are assured of His peace and guidance.

Don't be pulled in different directions or worried about a thing. Be saturated in prayer throughout each day, offering your faith-filled requests before God with overflowing gratitude. Tell him every detail of your life, then

God's wonderful peace that transcends human understanding, will make the answers known to you through Jesus Christ.

— PHILIPPIANS 4:6-7 TPT

8. He's your best friend! Psalm 23 is one of my favorite reminders that even in the darkest times, He lovingly leads us through to joy. We don't need to fear the future; we only need to trust His goodness.

YAHWEH is my best friend and my shepherd. I always have more than enough. He offers a resting place for me in his luxurious love. His tracks take me to an oasis of peace, near *the quiet brook of bliss*. That's where he restores and revives my life. He opens before me the right path and leads me along in his footsteps of righteousness so that I can bring honor to his name.

— PSALM 23:1-3 TPT

9. He's your victorious guide! How loving and reassuring it is that with Him as our guide, we have everything we need for life, strength, victory, belonging, restoration, hope, and peace.

Even when your path takes me through the valley of deepest darkness, fear will never conquer me, for you already have! Your authority is my strength and my peace. The comfort of your love takes away my fear. I'll never be lonely, for you are near.

— PSALM 23:4 TPT

10. He is for you! His goodness surrounds you always. You have the hope of life everlasting.

> You become my delicious feast even when my enemies dare to fight. You anoint me with the fragrance of your Holy Spirit; you give me all I can drink of you until my cup overflows. *So why would I fear the future?* Only goodness and tender love pursue me all the days of my life. Then afterward, when my life is through, I'll return to your glorious presence to be forever with you!

> — PSALM 23:5-6 TPT

11. He's concerned with your concerns! The simplicity and yet complexity of this verse overwhelms my heart. Take God at His Word. Give Him all your concerns. Let Him tenderly care for you; He promises He will do it.

> Pour out all your worries and stress upon him *and leave them there*, for he always tenderly cares for you.

> — 1 PETER 5:7 TPT

12. He's got all your needs covered! We can take each day as it comes. If we let Him permeate our lives and trust in Him, He promises provision and help for each day.

> What I'm trying to do here is to get you to relax, to not be so preoccupied with *getting,* so you can respond to God's *giving.* People who don't know God and the way he works fuss over these things, but you know both God and how he works. Steep your life in God-reality, God-initiative, God-provisions. Don't worry about missing out. You'll find all your everyday human concerns will be

met. Give your entire attention to what God is doing right now, and don't get worked up about what may or may not happen tomorrow. God will help you deal with whatever hard things come up when the time comes.

— MATTHEW 6:31-34 MSG

13. Whatever it is, don't panic! God promised He has got you!

I've picked you. I haven't dropped you. Don't panic. I'm with you. There's no need to fear for I'm your God. I'll give you strength. I'll help you. I'll hold you steady, keep a firm grip on you.

— ISAIAH 41:9-10 MSG

14. You are not alone! Trust the Lord for guidance; consult Him for every decision, big or small. He promises to lead you.

Trust in the Lord completely, and do not rely on your own opinions. With all your heart rely on him to guide you, and he will lead you in every decision you make. Become intimate with him in whatever you do, and he will lead you wherever you go.

— PROVERBS 3:5-6 TPT

15. This is the key to finding peace! Think on these things!

Finally, brothers and sisters, whatever is true, whatever is noble, whatever is right, whatever is pure, whatever is lovely, whatever is admirable—if anything is excellent or praiseworthy—think about such things... And the God of peace will be with you.

16. You don't have to fear! The God of the universe has you by the hand. Rest here; you can trust Him.

For I am the LORD your God who takes hold of your right hand and says to you, do not fear; I will help you.

— ISAIAH 41:13

17. He is faithful! His love and our hope are refilled every day. Circumstances won't overtake us as we wait in His presence. We can confidently expect breakthrough.

Because of the LORD's great love we are not consumed, for his compassions never fail. They are new every morning; great is your faithfulness. I say to myself, "The LORD is my portion; therefore, I will wait for him." The LORD is good to those whose hope is in him, to the one who seeks him.

— LAMENTATIONS 3:22-25

18. Breathe! It's important to find space that allows us to silence the noise of life so we can sit in His presence, read His Word, and pray. Do the little things that bring you joy and let Him remind you who He is.

Be still, and know that I am God.

— PSALM 46:10

19. He sees you! He promises healing, often not how or when

we expect, but He keeps His promises. His best is always worth waiting for.

I have heard your prayer and seen your tears; I will heal you.

— 2 KINGS 20:5

20. You have purpose (you are here by design, not by accident)! Great detail went into our stories before He even breathed life into us. We are here by design, and we matter so much to Him.

I knew you before I formed you in your mother's womb. Before you were born I set you apart and appointed you as my prophet to the nations.

— JEREMIAH 1:5 NLT

21. He loves you so much! His desire to have a relationship with us is so great that He willingly gave up His most precious Son to make it possible, and Jesus was willing to obey because He carries the heart of His Father. It's a gift freely given but at a great personal cost to Him. All He asks of us is to trust and believe.

For here is the way God loved the world—he gave his only, unique Son as a gift. So now everyone who believes in him will never perish but experience everlasting life.

— JOHN 3:16 TPT

22. Love without fear! God is love. He loves us toward the best version of ourselves and greater maturity in our faith. We do not

need to fear the tough things we face nor see them as punishment. In kindness and love, He holds onto us, walking next to us, giving us strength and, ultimately, victory over our circumstances.

> Love never brings fear, for fear is always related to punishment. But love's perfection drives the fear *of punishment far* from our hearts.
>
> — 1 JOHN 4:18 TPT

23. We have power over fear and torment! God has given us the Holy Spirit to minister His love and peace, giving us power over our accuser. We can ask the Holy Spirit to silence the voices that lie to us about the need to fear.

> For God has not given us a spirit of fear, but of power and of love and of a sound mind.
>
> — 2 TIMOTHY 1:7 NKJV

24. God's good character! God never acts out of harshness but in perfect love, which is full of grace and patience. He is both true and *the truth*.

> But Lord, your nurturing love is tender and gentle. You are slow to get angry yet so swift to show your faithful love. You are full of abounding grace and truth.
>
> — PSALM 86:15 TPT

25. He's the best leader! When we turn our hearts toward Him, inviting Him to lead the way, He promises us a hopeful future. He has the perfect road map.

"For I know the plans I have for you," says the LORD. "They are plans for good and not for disaster, to give you a future and a hope."

— JEREMIAH 29:11 NLT

26. Live in freedom! When Jesus becomes our Savior, the Holy Spirit lives within us. Where He dwells, there is full access to the power, strength, and peace we need to live free from concerns and anxieties.

Now, the "Lord" *I'm referring to* is the Holy Spirit, and wherever he is Lord, there is freedom.

— 2 CORINTHIANS 3:17 TPT

27. He brings joy! When we allow ourselves to believe in who He is and the delight He takes in us—when we begin trusting His promises and choosing to praise Him despite our circumstances—our hearts fill with gladness, joy enters our lives, and His perfect joy becomes our strength to ride out every storm.

The joy of the LORD is your strength.

— NEHEMIAH 8:10

28. Be strong and have courage! Be encouraged by who God says you are to Him and all He has freely given for you. You have nothing to fear. He promises to be with you wherever you go; He is always beside you.

Be strong and courageous. Do not be afraid; do not be discouraged, for the LORD your God will be with you wherever you go.

29. What a life He has for us! This verse summarizes my entire journey so far. Trust Him, giving Him full access to your heart, and let Him show you the purpose He has for your life. It will never bring disappointment.

> Keep trusting in the Lord and do what is right in his eyes. Fix your heart on the promises of God, and you will dwell in the land, feasting on his faithfulness. Find your delight and true pleasure in YAHWEH, and he will give you what you desire the most. Give God the right to direct your life, and as you trust him along the way, you'll find he pulled it off perfectly!

— PSALM 37:3-5 TPT

30. Step forward in confidence! Through Jesus, we have full access to all God's promises for our lives. We have hope for the future. We are assured of His love; He's our safe haven. Our circumstances will never overtake us. In Him, we are more than conquerors every day.

> We come closer to God and approach him with an open heart, fully convinced that nothing will keep us at a distance from him. For our hearts have been sprinkled with blood to remove impurity, and we have been freed from an accusing conscience. Now we are clean, unstained, and presentable to God inside and out! So now wrap your heart tightly around the hope that lives within us, knowing that God always keeps his promises!

— HEBREWS 10:22-23 TPT

ACKNOWLEDGMENTS

It goes without saying that without God's love and tender care and the guidance of the Holy Spirit through this journey, I wouldn't have arrived here at all, but there are also many people I need to thank for this finished book in your hands.

To my mum and dad, thank you for the example you set for me to always follow the Lord's path against all odds.

To my O.G. Bible study group, thank you for your unshakeable patience, prayers, and encouragement in so much of my life. Ladies, we can do hard things!

To my book club friends, thank you for taking a foreigner into your already established group and making me feel at home. Your acceptance, love, and support meant more than you'll ever know.

Lauren, when this project felt beyond my capabilities, you gave it fresh life so I could push to complete it. You gave your time and expertise so generously.

Lorraine, your wisdom, friendship, and encouragement are such a gift. I'm so grateful for you.

To my dearest UK friends, thank you for your excitement and encouragement for this project. I miss you all.

To the truly amazing Katie and all the team at Branch & Vine Publishing, thank you for patiently wading through that first long-winded draft—fashioned after my Irish storytelling roots —to make me sound better than I thought I could!

To my amazing HopeUC Nashville Hope at Home group, thank you for your prayers, support, and advice.

Last but never least, to my growing family, thank you for how you enrich my life with love, support, and adventures. I love you more than words can express. Especially to my long-suffering husband, thank you for your unconditional love and unwavering belief in me—we make a good team. I love you always.

ABOUT THE AUTHOR

Karen Thompson is an adventurer. Born and raised in Northern Ireland during "The Troubles," she later moved to England in her late teens to start a new life. Since then, her and her family have made their home in Tennessee, USA.

As a wife, mother, and grandmother, family has always been a high priority in all she has chosen to do. As a connector of people, faith and community are woven throughout Karen's story—whether it's volunteering at school boards, leading small groups, or inviting people to sit at her dining room table—her passion is creating opportunities where people are welcomed, stories are heard, laughter resounds, and friendships are made.

Along with her husband, Adrian, Karen is the co-founder of Ginger Daisy Ventures, which is a company committed to supporting and encouraging the development of Christian artists and songwriters across all genres through consultancy and management. To stay connected with Karen and learn more, please visit www.gingerdaisyventures.com.

instagram.com/streamsinthewildernessbook